MILLER'S

COLLECTING
FASHION & ACCESSORIES

First published in Great Britain in 2000 by Miller's, an imprint of
Octopus Publishing Group Limited

Miller's is a registered trademark of Octopus Publishing Group Limited

This revised edition published in 2013 by Bounty Books,
a division of Octopus Publishing Group Ltd,
Endeavour House, 189 Shaftesbury Avenue,
London WC2H 8JY

© 2000, 2013 Octopus Publishing Group Limited

Commissioning Editors: **Anna Sanderson, Elizabeth Stubbs**
Executive Art Editor: **Vivienne Brar**
Project Editor: **John Jervis**
Designers: **Dan Newman/Perfect Bound, Lucy Parissi**
Picture Research: **Denise Lalonde**
Production: **Nancy Roberts**
Special photography by **Steve Tanner**

The publishers will be grateful for any information that will assist them in keeping
future editions up to date. While every care has been exercised in the compilation of
this guide, neither the author not the publisher accept any liability for any financial or
other loss incurred arising from the use thereof, or the information contained herein.

A CIP record for this book is available from the British Library

ISBN 978-0-753723-67-8

Printed and bound in China

MILLER'S

COLLECTING
FASHION & ACCESSORIES

Carol Harris
General Editor: Madeleine Marsh

Contents

6 **Introduction**
10 **Chronology**

16 **Early Fashion**
18 Daywear
22 Eveningwear
24 Lingerie
26 Accessories
28 Menswear

30 **The Twenties**
32 Daywear
36 Eveningwear
38 Lingerie
40 Accessories
42 Menswear

44 **The Thirties**
46 Daywear
50 Eveningwear
52 Lingerie
54 Accessories
56 Menswear

58 **The Forties**
60 Daywear
64 Eveningwear
66 Lingerie
68 Accessories
70 Menswear

72 **The Fifties**
74 Daywear
78 Eveningwear
80 Lingerie
82 Accessories
84 Menswear

86 **The Sixties**
88 Daywear
92 Eveningwear
94 Lingerie
96 Accessories
98 Menswear

100 **The Seventies**
102 Daywear
106 Eveningwear
108 Lingerie
110 Accessories
112 Menswear
114 Unisex

116 **The Eighties**
118 Daywear
122 Eveningwear
124 Lingerie
126 Accessories
128 Menswear
130 Unisex

132 **The Nineties**
134 Daywear
138 Eveningwear
140 Lingerie
142 Accessories
144 Menswear
146 Unisex

148 **Useful addresses**
150 **Caring for
your collection**
151 **Bibliography**
152 **Glossary**
156 **Index**
160 **Acknowledgments**

Introduction

As a child, I loved delving in a dressing-up box filled with my mother's cast-offs, and I still enjoy wearing old clothes today. Collecting fashion is a very active pleasure. Unlike many other antiques, which often sit at home gathering dust, vintage clothes can be put on and shown off – they are the ultimate in portable collectables.

The satisfactions of collecting fashion are many. Clothes provide a direct link with the people of the past, and give a sense of living history. Try on an Edwardian coat, a 1920s flapper dress, a 1950s ball gown, or a 1960s mini-skirt, and you look, feel, and even walk differently. Over the years I have met a wide variety of costume collectors, and whilst some experiment with different periods, many focus on a specific decade that suits both their personality and their figure. Enthusiasts of the 1920s are often small and slight, 1950s fans are frequently curvaceous, while 1960s dressers tend to be enviably long and leggy. There are those that go all the way, ensuring that their underwear, outerwear, hairstyle, make-up, and accessories are all perfectly in period. Others, myself included, mix and match the old and new: you can wear a 1930s shirt with a pair of jeans, or a 1970s coat with a modern dress, and a vintage handbag can provide the perfect complement to any outfit.

Having a century of styles to choose from is a liberating experience. Rather than slavishly following the latest look, you can choose to wear whatever you like – paradoxically, if you dress from the past, it is almost impossible to be unfashionable. Shopping is no longer a chore, but an adventure: you never know what you will find when rifling through the rails at a vintage-clothes store, but it will almost certainly be interesting. Antique clothes are usually beautifully made (or else they would not have survived the decades), and can also be surprisingly affordable. My own favourite is a 1950s dress, a miracle of boning and netting, with its cotton print still fresh as a daisy, which cost me next to nothing at a charity shop. Above all, they are fun to wear: go to a party in vintage clothes and your outfit will be unique. People will come up and ask you about it – antique clothes can be a great ice-breaker!

Collecting fashion is a comparatively recent hobby. For my grandmother's generation, the idea of wearing something second-hand would have been incomprehensible, even shameful. It was not until the 1960s that old clothes became a fashion statement rather than a mark of poverty, and today the market is booming, with growing numbers of dealers, auction houses, and collectors. Many of today's leading designers are inspired by the fashion of the past, and sometimes, by wearing a period original, you can find yourself in the vanguard of modern fashion.

Miller's Collecting Fashion & Accessories provides a guide to a century of style, and is a comprehensive introduction to vintage costume, from dresses and lingerie to shoes and bags. Each section provides historical information about the major influences and trends of the decade, together with practical advice on care and condition, and expert buying tips for collectors. Every item shown comes complete with a suggested price range which reflects current market values, and indicates what you might expect to pay for a garment at specialist dealers or period fashion fairs, not what you might sell it for to a dealer.

Our thanks to all the dealers, collectors, and specialists who contributed to this book. We hope that you enjoy it, and that next time you go shopping for clothes, you won't forget the wardrobe of the past.

Madeleine Marsh
General Editor

*Four 1940s supermodels who have the looks and figures to show off Christian Dior's New Look.
Most women of this time could only aspire to this shape, and dream of the luxury that the
style represented. As far as Dior was concerned, it was a case of everything to excess, in the
silhouette, the materials, and the prices of the garments.*

Fifty years on, these supermodels show that the tall, willowy frame is still in fashion. These supermodels (left to right: Linda Evangelista, Cindy Crawford, Naomi Campbell, and Christy Turlington) are at the pinnacle of their success: Linda Evangelista spoke for the most famous when she allegedly remarked that she didn't get out of bed for less than $10,000 a day.

1900

- Edward VII succeeds his mother, Queen Victoria, in 1901, setting the tone for the advent of ostentatious Edwardian styles.
- The hourglass or "S"-shape silhouette results in years of agony, as women resemble well-upholstered armchairs.
- Ladies change their clothes several times a day assisted by a maid, an essentia member of the household.
- Corset manufacturers are clear about the purpose of their garments, which have names like "Adjusto" and "Reduso".
- Middle and working-class men adopt the three-piece suit for work and leisure.
- Pau Poiret's "empire line" and his "hobble" skirts liberate women from corsets, but tether ankles thus restricting movement in the legs.
- The top-heavy look takes over, with padded bust, straight skirts, and huge, "Merry Widow"-style hats.
- Serge Diaghilev's *Ballets Russes* tours Europe bringing its designers, notably Leon Bakst, to prominence.
- Art Nouveau inspires softer, romantic designs by Klimt and Lanvin. Fortuny's dresses are inspired by Classica sculpture, the Aesthetic movement and Renaissance art.
- Narrow skirts, often with fishtail-shape trains, are popular. Women begin to reject the restricting lines of the hourglass shape – lampshade-style tunics and tight skirts are the choices of the fashionable.
- The influence of the Suffragettes, the Dress Reform movement, and the increased involvement of women in sports such as cycling and swimming provoke demand for practica clothes.

1910

- The Tango is fashionable, encouraging a trend for dresses with side slits and roomier bodices which allow freer movement.
- Lampshade-style tunics reach new extremes in the collections of 1913.
- Artificia silk hosiery and, later, knitwear, is produced commercially for the first time.
- Coco Chane opens her first shop, in Deauville, France.
- The long hot summer of 1914 is a prelude to the outbreak of World War I, with fashionable young women dressing in girlish,

◤ *Two fans from the early years of the century*

- romantic lawn dresses, accompanied by men in their straw boaters and striped blazers.
- The USA, less affected by wartime shortages, emerges for the first time as a major fashion trendsetter.
- The high rate of casualties among young men fighting the war gives rise to the term "the Lost Generation".
- Wartime promotes sober lines and colours, and encourages clothes which serve several purposes, especially as women volunteer for war work.
- As the war progresses, women adopt more masculine styles. By 1918, the wearing of make-up by women is widespread, if not yet widely accepted.
- The Russian Revolution creates shock waves in Europe and America.
- The 'flu epidemic, helped in its spread through Europe and America by returning troops, kills more than the total number of casualties during World War I.
- As the 1920s begin, there are a million cars on the road worldwide – the pace of life is becoming noticeably faster.

1920

- Tutankhamun's tomb is discovered in 1922 by Howard Carter, provoking fascination with "Egyptian" styling.
- "Jazz Babies" copy the bobbed hair and rouged cheeks of film star Clara Bow, whose social life is documented in lurid detail by popular newspapers.
- The Prince of Wales, Douglas Fairbanks, and Rudolf Valentino are the icons who influence men's clothing.
- Sports clothes set fashion trends, especially those worn by stars of tennis and aviation such as Helen Wills Moody, Amy Johnson, and Amelia Earhart.
- Noel Coward's play *The Vortex* shocks with its references to loose morals and drugs.
- The worsening economic climate in Europe fuels an atmosphere of decadence and uncertainty, summed up in Pabst's 1928 film, *Pandora's Box*, staring Louise Brooks.
- F. Scott Fitzgerald sets the tone of the time in his novel, *The Great Gatsby*.
- Elastic and plastics replace whalebone and padding in lingerie, and brassières become bras by the end of the 1920s.
- Paris is the centre for artists and musicians, especially black Americans such as dancer Josephine Baker, prevented by prejudice from developing similar

A top hat from 1900–20

- careers in their home country.
- Failure of 1926 General Strike in Britain causes some to think society remains unchanged, and others to believe a Russian-style revolution is at hand.
- The Wall Street Crash of 1929 brings the Depression to the USA.
- Coco Chanel and Jean Patou bring waistlines back to their natural position in their collections of autumn 1929.

1930

- The frantic frivolity of the 1920s is replaced by the cool and alluring styles of the "Smart Set".
- Hemlines are lowered and bias-cutting, in which fabrics cling closely to the hips before flowing in a full skirt to the ground, becomes almost standard for evening and day dresses.
- Prohibition of alcohol in America ends in 1933, but night-clubs known as "speakeasys" continue to flourish.
- Hitler becomes German Chancellor in 1933 – the triumph of Nazism provokes an exodus of leading figures in the arts to the rest of Europe and to America.
- The Hays Office is established to curb the excesses of Hollywood films, while

Edwardian corset with decorative borders

Driving gauntlets from the 1930s

Chronology

morality clauses in contracts seek to restrict the private lives of stars.

- Greta Garbo and Katharine Hepburn wear men's styles, encouraging the popularity of trousers among women.
- Health and fitness are in vogue in Europe and America, and a tan becomes a fashion accessory for the first time.
- The Spanish Civil War of 1936–39 acts in many respects as a dress rehearsal for World War II.
- Edward VIII abdicates, marries Wallis Simpson, and settles in France, where they shop and entertain on a lavish scale.
- As the 1930s progress, romanticism takes over from subtlety and sophistication among leading Parisian couturiers.
- Nylon stockings are produced commercially in America in the late 1930s, but European women have to wait until American GIs start bringing them over in the early 1940s.

◄ *Nylon stockings from the 1940s by Elsa Schiaparelli*

1940

- Clothing is rationed: materials such as rubber, elastic, and silk are requisitioned for military purposes.
- Shortages make both bias-cutting and silk underwear fondly recalled but unattainable memories.
- The 1941 Utility scheme, providing good quality but economically produced garments, proves so successful that it is extended to other common items such as furniture.
- The British Government urges women to "Go Through Your Wardrobe and Make Do and Mend", while in the USA, women are urged to support the war effort by spending as much as possible on their clothes.
- The USA enters the war in 1941 after the Japanese bomb Pearl Harbour.
- Hats and fur are neither rationed nor brought under the Utility scheme. But they soon become too expensive, and difficult to find for those without the necessary wealth or connections.
- Paris is finally liberated in 1944, and soon becomes subject to the same restrictions as the other Allies for the first time since World War II began.
- The war ends but shortages worsen, as Europe slowly gets back on its economic feet.
- Christian Dior launches the Corolle look in 1947, popularly called the New Look, flying in the face of worsening peacetime shortages and thus provoking widespread outrage.

1950

- Greater affluence is accompanied by the growing influence of American styling and culture: television replaces cinema as the opium of the masses, and many European homes have refrigerators, washing machines and cars.
- Elvis Presley makes his first outrageous appearance with his white boy's version of black American music. Bill Haley and the Comets have a similar effect with *Rock Around the Clock*.
- Italian styling, especially on men's suits and women's leather shoes and bags, is the ultimate in sophistication.
- The Sac dress, the sheath, the "A"-line, and the "H"-line all enjoy brief moments at the centre of the fashion stage.
- Fur is fashionable, especially in extreme forms such as the mink bikini modelled by British film star Diana Dors, one of many actresses who followed in the footsteps of Marilyn Monroe.
- American designer Clare McCardell makes an impact on Europe with her "sportswear" designs.
- American culture makes both "bomber" jackets and casual shirts in bright colours or prints popular with men.
- Teenagers are identifiable as a distinct group for the first time, with their own, growing spending power.
- In the film *The Wild One*, Marlon Brando broods and pouts as the archetypal rebellious teenager.
- The Cold War and McCarthyism epitomize the atomic age and the fears it holds. In Cuba, the Communist overthrow of the Batista regime provokes a brief revival of the zoot suit and loose-fitting gaucho trousers.
- Stiletto heels are soon banned from some public buildings because of the damage to linoleum floors, but the new heel bars do a roaring trade.

1960

- Mary Quant establishes the Ginger Group, selling mass-produced clothes direct to people on the High Street, without an initial launch in a fashionable and exclusive salon.
- Mini-skirts and dresses worn with boots, large caps, short hair, and heavy eye make-up are all fashionable.
- Courrèges launches his Space Age collection and Paco Rabanne his metal dresses in the mid-1960s.
- Vidal Sassoon introduces his layered bob, a hairstyle emphasizing the geometric shape of Space Age style.
- Twiggy is the decade's leading model: gawky, knock-kneed, and androgynous, her youth and working-class London accent are new elements of 1960s style.
- The boutiques of King's Road and Carnaby Street turn "Swinging London" into the fashion capital of the world.
- The Beatles set trends, initially for "moptop" haircuts and sharp, collarless, Pierre Cardin suits, and then for bright satins and long hair following the release in 1967 of their *Sergeant Pepper* LP.
- "Flower Power" reaches its height in 1967 as the Beatles visit the Maharishi in India, and Timothy Leary encourages people to tune in, turn on, and drop out.

◤ *Embroidered cardigan from the 1950s*

➤ *1960s evening dress with full skirt*

Chronology

- The space race culminates in 1969 with Neil Armstrong walking on the moon.
- Recreational drug use has a high profile: calls to legalize cannabis and other drugs, notably LSD, attract widespread debate among all parts of society.
- The hippy movement encourages a general fascination with the East, and with ethnically inspired designs.
- Growing protests against the Vietnam War in the USA and Britain, coupled with riots in Paris in 1968, are accompanied by a new fondness for working-class and military chic.
- The Women's Liberation movement gains ground in the USA, but it is not until the publication of Germaine Greer's *The Female Eunuch* that, after a decade notable in retrospect for its overt sexism, serious questions about the lot of women are asked.

1970

- Uncertainty at the directions of street-led fashion prompts a range of styles in the shops, including the mini, maxi and midi (mid-calf) lengths.
- Discos encourage fashions for satin hot pants, afro hair and stretchy tops.
- Millions of young westerners follow the hippy trail to India and Nepal.

- The oil crisis of 1973 throws the Western world into recession. Second-hand clothing becomes so popular it develops a style of its own – "Oxfam Chic".
- Japanese designers such as Yamamoto and Kenzo develop a new approach to cut and styling – the "Big Look" of oversized shirts, coats, and cowboy boots.
- *Saturday Night Fever* results in "Medallion Man", with his droopy moustache, satin shirt slashed to the waist, and very tight-waisted, flared trousers.
- Clothes worn by American black leaders, and by Richard Rowntree as Shaft in the "Blaxploitation" films, influence styles among all ethnic groups.
- "Glam rock" brings androgynous styles to prominence. Unisex fashions become mainstream, especially denim jeans, platform shoes, hats, and other accessories.
- Logos and trademarks decorate everything from T-shirts to shoes.
- The fresh, anarchic street-style of punks is hugely influential, and its foremost designers help lead mainstream fashion for the rest of the century.

◄ *Bright 1970s bra*

▲ *Ethnic-style shirt from the 1970s*

1980

- Margaret Thatcher and Ronald Reagan are unlikely fashion trendsetters, setting a tone of ostentatious display, and giving rise to the "Yuppies", young professionals whose moral code was founded on the rule of market forces alone.
- The Soviet invasion of Afghanistan provokes a boycott of the Moscow Olympics by the USA, but by the end of the decade, communism was collapsing throughout Eastern Europe.
- American soap operas *Dallas* and *Dynasty*, based on wealthy families having a miserable time, set fashion styles, with padded shoulders, pageboy hairstyles, and power suits.
- The engagement of Lady Diana Spencer to the Prince of Wales establishes her as a fashion leader.
- Recession provokes riots in the streets of Britain. Equality for homosexuals, women, and ethnic minorities is vigorously promoted in London and other cities, influencing fashions of the time.
- Designer labels become fashion essentials, as fashion houses make millions licensing everything from perfume to underwear.

- Environmental concerns perpetuate the fascination with home crafts and recycling, which had been the focus of radical movements in the 1970s.
- AIDS (acquired immune deficiency syndrome) dominates the health concerns of sexually active people, especially homosexual men.
- Economic recession sets in at the end of the decade, encouraging the counter-culture of the New Age movement.
- British designers such as Vivienne Westwood and John Galliano are leaders in radical fashion, while US styles, such as those of Ralph Lauren and Calvin Klein, promote more sober, wearable ranges.

1990

- Army surplus is in fashion, this time from the unwanted stocks held by armies of previously communist-led countries in Eastern Europe.
- The Prince and Princess of Wales divorce. Diana, Princess of Wales, as she is now known, wears stilettos at every opportunity and develops a more subtle, sophisticated style. A charity auction of her dresses, held in the USA just before her death, raises enormous sums for charity.
- Monsanto, previously known for its synthetic fabrics, becomes best known for its role in developing genetically modified food.
- The Internet, originally developed for US Military Intelligence, becomes a global link between computer-owning individuals across the planet.
- The lobby for equal rights for disabled people provokes designers to think more radically, and velcro becomes a mainstream feature for fastenings.
- Alexander McQueen and John Galliano are in charge of design at Givenchy and Dior respectively.
- Designer labels are still essential wear among the "glitterati" but, with the huge boom in media sports coverage, team strips now become the casual shirt of choice for many.
- The trend for comfort in fashion continues – men in particular wear easy-care shorts and T-shirts in styles identical to those worn by their children.
- Young people who go clubbing develop their own vastly differing styles of dress, unintentionally assisted by door staff, who allow entry only to those dressed according to their code.
- As the decade and the century draw to a close, people start purchasing glittering and glitzy clothes to celebrate the start of the year 2000.

↖ *Two typical bags from the 1980s*

↖ *1990s platform trainers*

Early Fashion

At the start of the 20th century, women sat stiffly in their boned and corseted gowns, presenting the favoured "S"-shape, with full, shelf-like bosoms, small waists, and full hips. The Edwardian lady changed her floor-length gowns several times a day, whether for shopping, luncheon, evening dinner, receiving guests, or taking tea. Fashionable women, however, were known as "Gibson Girls" after the cartoons of Charles Dana Gibson – they wore bustles and shorter skirts, and had hair piled up in chignons under plumed hats, and rode bicycles. In 1910 the designer Paul Poiret encouraged women to abandon corsets in favour of his "hobble" skirts, while his décolleté dresses, with their skirts drawn in tight above the ankle, left no room for the traditional voluminous underwear. Designers, notably Fortuny and Lanvin, also drew inspiration from Art Nouveau and the Far East for their loose, softly draped garments. During World War I, women's fashions adopted a more masculine tone, and sober colours became standard for daywear. The shortage of fabrics also popularized outfits that could be worn for a variety of occasions, and the ritual of changing several times daily declined. And, as the 1920s loomed, skirts were already getting shorter.

Daywear

The wide range of dress shapes at the turn of the century was indicative of social changes. The hourglass figure, layered clothing, and the "S"-shape all held sway until about 1906. Many younger people, however, reacted against constriction in fashion, and the dominance of corsetry began to wane. Revivals of Classicism, a renewed interest in the Pre-Raphaelites, and demands for a more tailored look all flourished. Russian styling was encouraged by the success of the *Ballets Russes*, which toured Europe in 1909. As war threatened, feminine, even girlish styles came into vogue. Department stores, well-established in the USA during the previous century, became popular in Europe – their spectacular window displays and huge ranges of garments proved irresistible. Despite the American influence on retail trends, fashion in the USA was generally thought to be in need of education – especially from titled European ladies such as Lady Duff Cooper (1863–1935), who opened her own salons in New York under the name "Lucile".

◄ The green, embroidered motifs on this silk dress recall William Morris (1834–96), but this design is also similar to those of Charles Rennie Mackintosh (1868–1928). The loose style is easy to move around in, and is rather more practical than the "hobble" skirts of Paul Poiret (1879–1944), who worked with leading Paris couturiers Worth and Doucet, before opening his own house in 1908.

Grey silk dress   **£120–180/$200–300**

◄ Motoring was the new craze of the wealthy in the early 20th century. People who changed into special clothes to drink tea would, of course, have clothing specifically for driving. Fashion aside, the roads of this time were dusty and dirty, and not designed for the average car, so full-length coats covered as much as possible. Goggles and thickly veiled hats, often tied around the neck, would accompany such coats. Although it has some damage, this is a lovely and historic example from the beginnings of the motor car.

Motoring coat   **£350–450/$500–600**

➤ This dress, with its "leg of mutton" sleeves, full skirt, and tiny waist, is typical of styling at the start of the 20th century. It shows how everyday wear would, to modern eyes, be very highly decorated. Great attention was paid to cuffs. They would feature details such as the bows shown here, and would sometimes finish in a point on the back of the hand.

£700–1000/$1000–1500   *Grey dress*

➤ Cotton lawn was popular for both under and outer garments, and now evokes images of long hot summers and young ladies taking tea. This tiered dress is a comparatively practical example of the tunic style, taken to extremes in the years before World War I, which culminated in a lampshade shape, worn over draped or fishtail skirts.

£350–450/$500–600   *White dress*

➤ A wonderful layered dress: the black taffeta rests on a layer of machine lace. The back view is shown here to give an idea of the trailing skirt. Such trailing and floor-length dresses inevitably became very dirty – trimmings on both under-wear and outerwear were often detachable to make cleaning easier.

Black lace dress   **£1000–1500/$1500–2000**

◄ This loose dress has a simple, plain line, but a considerable amount of decoration has been incorporated, including the self-covered buttons. This less formal style features abundant lace trimmings, which mimic the decoration used on underwear. Pale colours, especially lilacs and greys, were very popular at the beginning of the 20th century, and the high-waisted style of this dress was popular from about 1907.

£250–300/$400–500

Pink cotton dress

➤ A beautiful dress suitable for croquet, popular in the gardens of wealthy people by 1900. High necks were common in daywear, in contrast to the décolleté style preferred in the evening. Lawn or muslin dresses in virginal white such as this were part of every young lady's wardrobe immediately prior to World War I, when the vogue for girlish innocence was at its height.

£350–400/$500–600   *White dress*

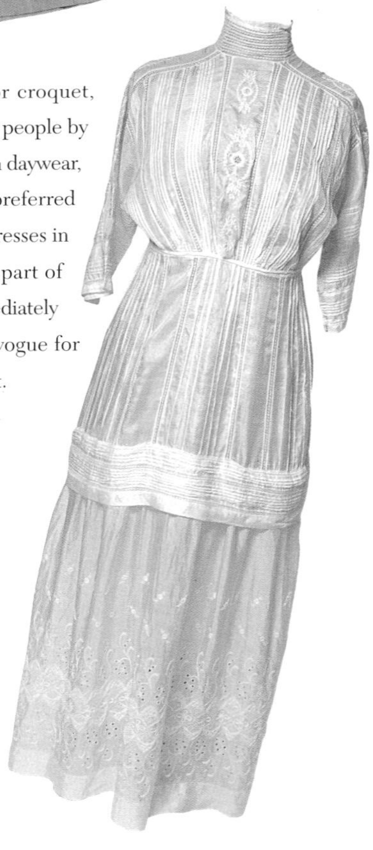

◄ The draped bust and flowing skirt were classic features of the post-Edwardian era. Hats became smaller after the excesses of the cartwheel styles, but the ostrich plume endured. This one-piece dress, from the collection of the Victoria & Albert Museum in London, is in near perfect condition. Skirts and separate blouses were fashionable until 1909, when the one-piece dress reasserted itself.

Dress and hat   **£3000–4000/$4500–5500**

⬆ Suit jackets had a soft line at the waist and bust. Full skirts allowed for easier movement, and the cashmere mixture of this one means that, even today, the fabric has "bounce". Influences such as the Suffrage movement, dance crazes, especially for the Tango, and increased participation in sports, encouraged a demand for practical clothes. Skirts could be split, and became slightly shorter, revealing the feet, as the two figures on these pages show.

Suit   **£350–450/$500–600**

➤ A stunning ensemble: the fine detail and hand-sewn work on this dress are sure signs that it was made to measure for a wealthy client. The bows and slits in the bodice and sleeves are very intricate, and the lace panel is exotically patterned. Women wore long gloves, usually in fine kid, at all times of the day, changing them to match their outfits. The hat is typical of the enormous and highly decorated styles of the early 1900s. Items from this period should not be worn – top-quality examples are best displayed on dummies.

£2000–3000/$3000–4000   *White dress and hat*

Eveningwear

Eveningwear in the Edwardian era gave full rein to opulence and display. Low-cut necklines allowed space for abundant jewellery, feather boas, and chokers. The stage had an enormous influence on fashion – many designers, including Paul Poiret, also worked on costumes for ballet. In France, the tubular silhouette and the "Directoire" style resulted in evening ensembles featuring beaded tunics over high-waisted, heavily draped undergowns. With its Empire still intact and its economy flourishing, Britain was at its most confident – the upheavals of wartime were yet to dispel the certainties of life. However the horrors of World War I discouraged the vogue for show – in Europe, it was thought unpatriotic to display wealth. Women took on work previously done by men, and wanted clothes they could wear in a variety of settings. *Vogue* reported the emergence of the "restaurant gown", which could be worn in the afternoon or for dinner at home. As the War ended, however, brighter colours and more decorative styles re-emerged, and hemlines once again trailed behind women venturing out for an evening at the opera or the theatre.

◄ Edwardians were enthusiastic advocates of dining out. Despite some damage, this is a wonderful example of the Edwardian dinner dress. It has beautiful, bugle beadwork on an abundance of lace decoration. The shaped hem is an interesting feature which adds to the value. Around 1910, hems were raised and feet became visible. Long dresses often had detachable additions, called furbelows, fixed to the hem, which helped to protect the dress from damage and dirt.

Dinner dress   **£1000–1500/$1500–2000**

➤ This magnificent dress shows the Edwardian taste for decoration and display at its height. The rich brocade materials and centre panel are balanced by heavily worked sleeves and shoulders. The wearer would have her hair dressed with large jewels or a tiara – Queen Alexandra, a noted beauty, inspired a fashion for heavily jewelled chokers which extended down the neck on to the chest in low-cut dresses such as the one shown here.

£2000–3000/$3000–4000

Brocade dress

▲ Wartime encouraged informality and looser styling in eveningwear, and, as war broke out, trimmings of lace and feathers fell out of favour. Even so, beaded tops such as this one in silk chiffon were extensively decorated. Black was a common choice for all times of the day, as many were bereaved, and rules about mourning clothes relaxed. Evening skirts became shorter towards the end of the war, although after 1918 longer styles with panniers briefly became popular again.

£300–400/$450–550

Beaded top

▼ Popular actresses and singers such as the "Gaiety Girls" set fashion trends for Edwardian society, and this sumptuous dress, with its low décolleté and long train, typifies the high style of the time. This example is made-to-measure, but department stores now sold ready-made dresses for day and evening, as well as having their own dressmaking departments.

£1500–2000/$2200–3200

Mauve dress

◄ A comparatively reserved dress: the deep "V" at the top, with an inset panel of contrasting material, became especially popular from 1911, as did side slits and loose-cut sleeves to aid dancing. Evening bags, like this valuable silver-mesh example with an amethyst clasp, are especially collectable if they retain contents such as coin purses.

Dress   **£1200–1800/$1800–2200**   *Evening bag*   **£300–400/$450–550**

Lingerie

After the rather plain undergarments of the Victorian era, underwear at the start of the 20th century was made to be both seen and heard. Lace and ribbon trimmings were visible beneath dresses, and petticoats in taffeta, silk, and satin would rustle alluringly as the wearer moved. The hourglass figure was slowly replaced by an emphasis on the bust to the exclusion of all else, making women seem top-heavy, even crab-like. There was no shame in artifice: exercise was unseemly, and also of little practical use for most women – the desired waist size was around 53–64cm (21–25in), achievable only with corsetry to anyone who possessed the required shelf-like bust. Those with sufficiently small hips, on the other hand, had to achieve the correct shape in the bosom with masses of padding. So the standard set of underwear might start with the chemise, corset, and knickers, then the camisole and petticoats. Combinations of knickers and chemise were an alternative under the corset. It is no surprise that Paul Poiret's "empire line", and the looser clothing inspired by Art Nouveau and by Eastern influences, were liberating for fashionable women, enabling them to breathe freely at last.

◄ The camisole, often highly decorated with lace and ribbon, was worn over a corset and gathered or cut to fit at the waist. The sleeveless and low-cut style is familiar today, but high necks, puff sleeves, and lace yokes were also popular. This example, with its beautiful buttons and lace trim, is typical. The style has often been revived, for example in the 1970s by Laura Ashley as a summer blouse.

Camisole **£150–500/$220–280**

◄ For daywear, knickers often had buttons on a band at the back and the knees. Drawstrings were an alternative, but elastic began to replace these by 1914. French knickers and divided skirts were left ungathered at the knees, and in spite of the warmth of layers of petticoats, fleecy-lined knickers were also popular.

£80–120/$120–180 *Knickers*

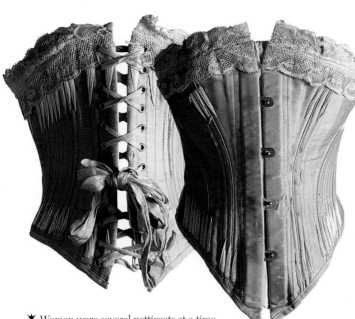

◄ Corsets came in many colours and fabrics – satin, silk, brocade, and coutil, a variety of twill. Decorative borders and motifs were common, and whalebone was still the shaper of choice. Corsets were dangerously restrictive – "Reduso" corsets promised to "reduce the hips and abdomen from one to five inches without straps or other injurious attachments", and one style promised the "stout woman the graceful lines of her slender sisters."

£400–500/$600–800 *Corsets (each)*

✦ Women wore several petticoats at a time, and the top layer was known as the underskirt. Petticoats were often lace or ribbon-trimmed and could be luxurious. From about 1908 the move towards looser dresses which revealed the shape of the thighs meant that petticoats were no longer essential: more daring followers of fashion did not even have their dresses lined.

Petticoat **£80–120/$120–180**

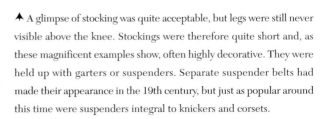

▲ A glimpse of stocking was quite acceptable, but legs were still never visible above the knee. Stockings were therefore quite short and, as these magnificent examples show, often highly decorative. They were held up with garters or suspenders. Separate suspender belts had made their appearance in the 19th century, but just as popular around this time were suspenders integral to knickers and corsets.

Stockings (per pair) **£50–80/$80–120**

Accessories

The Edwardian lady chose accessories to match the opulence of her outfits. Domestic help was relatively inexpensive at this time, so even a moderate, middle-class household could afford a full complement of servants. Dressing was never a solitary experience: the lady's maid would fetch and carry for her mistress, making sure her clothes were well looked after and clean (which helps to explain their excellent condition today). She would also dress the elaborate hairstyles, deal with rows of unreachable buttons or hooks and eyes, and fasten the tight corsets. Women wore enormous hats, held in place by gigantic hatpins. These were driven into hair which, itself long enough to sit on, was dressed in elaborate styles with false pieces, called rats, and padding. Feathers, flowers, fruit, and stuffed birds on hats, fur trimmings on muffs and cuffs, the ensemble finished off with a stole of fox, musquash,squirrel, coney, or even skunk, all gave rise to what we might think of today as the menagerie look.

➤ The parasol was an essential accessory, as a ruddy complexion marked one as a woman who worked. Those able to concentrate their energies on their appearance would have a number of parasols in colours and fabrics which matched their summer dresses. This beautiful parasol in sprigged organdie is in excellent condition, even down to the tassle on the handle. Parasols often have rust marks, which are impossible to remove completely.

Parasol   **£150–200/$180–220**

➤ An excellent pair of patent-leather boots, these have the typical pointed toes of the period. Boots to mid-calf were worn, especially in winter, by fashionable ladies. Louis and Cuban heels of low to medium height were popular, so shoes were ostensibly comfortable, but the restrictions of underwear meant that women could not walk naturally, while running was something no lady even dreamed of doing!

£300–400/$450–550
Patent-leather boots

➤ Fans are lovely to collect and were popular until the 1920s. Feathered fans were taken to dinner or the theatre, and had decorative and practical uses: women were liable to fainting, especially in restrictive under-wear, and a pale complexion was also idealized – patent cures for blushing were plentiful if ineffectual, and a fan could be relied upon to conceal the face in an embarrassing moment.

£150–200/$220–280   *Feather fan*

£100–150/$150–200   *Rose fan*

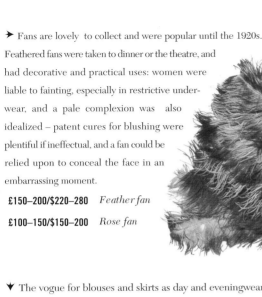

✦ The vogue for blouses and skirts as day and eveningwear made belts essential, adding emphasis to the waistline. Belts were often heavy and decorative, and, like this black-beaded evening version, were slung low round the hips with tassles hanging down the centre of the skirt, emphasizing the thighs. This belt also features an Art Nouveau-inspired design in green celluloid, an early plastic which was heavy and brittle. Feather boas were immensely popular – this one, also for eveningwear, has weighted tassles to keep it in place.

£60–80/$80–120   *Metal belt*

£180–220/$220–280   *Feather boa*

£200–300/$300–400   *Beaded belt*

✦ This style of mesh evening bag was hugely popular. It could not carry much – visiting cards, lipstick, rouge, a powder puff, and a coin purse, perhaps. Make-up was generally frowned upon, but women's emancipation, silent films stars such as Theda Bara, and exotic, eastern styling, made it acceptable as the 1920s approached.

Purse   **£120–180/$180–220**

27

Menswear

If the "Gay Nineties" suggests that the last decade of the 19th century was something of a party, then the host was definitely "Bertie", Prince of Wales. When he became King Edward VII, in 1901, he perpetuated his playboy image, and his influence on male fashion was wide ranging. Trouser creases and turn-ups, spats, Homburgs and Tyrolean hats, walking canes, ties, and cravats were a few of the innovations he popularized. The early decades of the 20th century were most notable for the rise of the lounge or business suit. Whether single or double breasted, the suit worn by working-class and middle-class men had a waistcoat and a three or four-buttoned jacket, with a ticket pocket. The Edwardian Dandy wore striped shirts in taffeta, wool, silk, or cotton, and, in cold weather, Chesterfield overcoats with velvet collars. Older men still wore frock coats for work, while the better-off wore them in the evening too – the new dinner jackets were too informal for traditionalists. Shoes and half boots began to replace boots, a trend encouraged by the popularity of spats.

◄ Most men could afford to dress only in the most sober colours, and many others chose to do so, aspiring to look like the archetypal gentleman. But those with the means and the inclination often dressed in vibrant colours and fabrics, of which this waistcoat is a magnificent example. For the fashion-conscious of the Edwardian era, it was considered stylish to make a great show of one's wealth – men would often choose to emphasize their well-fed frames by draping their watch chains across their chest and into the opposing pockets of their waistcoats.

£300–400/$450–550 *Waistcoat*

▼ Smoking was an almost exclusively male pastime – in public at least. Many developed the habit in "the Colonies", and also smoked cannabis, which was legal until 1928. As this smoking cap shows, the Eastern influence did not stop with Turkish tobacco – such a hat might well be worn with a velvet smoking jacket by the Edwardian gentleman. Cigarettes, cigars, cheroots, and all kinds of pipe tobaccos were common, as were smoking accessories such as lighters and cigarette cases.

£80–120/$120–180 *Smoking cap*

↘ London tailors set the style for menswear, just as Paris couturiers set the fashion for women. The Dandy shown here has the low-cut lapels, spats, cravat, cane, and collar all typical of the fashionable and wealthy Edwardian man. His trousers are narrow cut in the leg but generous in the seat, a style known as peg-top. Suits in velveteen were worn by the clothes-conscious man, but serge was the popular choice for most others. In the USA, men's suits were noticeably more colourful and less formal than in Europe. The customs and habits of immigrant communities, coupled with the need, away from the developed cities of the East Coast, for clothing that was essentially hardwearing and practical, gave rise to great diversity in style. In America, even a gentleman wore clothes that were cut for comfort and movement.

£1500–2000/$2200–3200   *Suit*

↓ The early 1900s was the time when the bowler hat (know in America as the Derby) became popular. Even so, the top hat retained its pre-eminence among traditionalists and the upper classes, and the silk version was still essential for eveningwear. The most popular hats worn at other times included caps, which at last achieved some respectability as fashion items, deerstalkers, Homburgs, and straw boaters. There was some dispute over whether a two-tone ribbon was acceptable on the latter in place of a plain black one – the former only gradually achieved respectability.

£100–150/$150–200   *Top hat*

The Twenties

Mention the 1920s and the flapper instantly comes to mind, with her short hair and her straight dress featuring a dropped waist and daringly short skirt, and perhaps revealing a glimpse of coloured silk stockings. The term was used in the 1890s to describe young prostitutes, but in the 1920s, according to The Long Weekend by Robert Graves and Alan Hodge, she was 'a comradely, sporting, active young woman who would ride on the "flapper bracket" of a motor cycle'. The straight, boyish lines of female fashion revealed the influence of the streamlined modernism of Art Deco. Easy-care, easy-wear designs were made possible by advances in manufacturing and fabrics, and there was a demand for clothes which reflected changes in women's lifestyles after World War I. Many more chose to work. They smoked, wore trousers, and, in 1928, were given the vote in Britain on the same terms as men. This was a modern age, when social upheaval, sparked by the futility of "the Great War", was matched by huge technological advances. Radio and film provided affordable and exciting forms of mass entertainment, and everything screen idols such as Rudolph Valentino and Greta Garbo wore or did was of interest to their fans.

Daywear

Separates were an essential part of the modern woman's wardrobe during the 1920s. Coco Chanel (1883–1971) began her hugely influential career by popularizing the jersey suit, with its free-flowing lines and easy movement, and in 1921 she introduced her famous "No.5" perfume. Tennis stars such as Suzanne Lenglen and Helen Wills Moody were the sporting heroines of the decade – when Jean Patou (1889–1936) sent Lenglen onto the courts at Wimbledon in a short, pleated, sleeveless dress, a fashion revolution began. Sweaters and skirts in matching or tonal colours also remained popular throughout the decade. British fashion developed a reputation for well cut, practical clothes – Norman Hartnell (1901–79), later couturier to Queen Elizabeth II, opened his first shop in 1927. Inexpensive versions of the latest fashions were now freely available from department stores, which, although they had been in existence on high streets since the 18th century and were flourishing in America, finally came into their own in Britain only after World War I.

◄ Artificial silk wool was just one of a wide range of knitting yarns available during the inter-war years. This blue, beige, and black "art silk" cardigan was machine knitted, and the blue borders on the pockets and the collar are in rayon jersey. The value is lessened by damage to the back. The silk blouse has typical 1920s-style faggoting, and the overall effect emphasizes the long line created between the shoulder and the hip.

£50–80/$80–120   *Cream blouse*

£40–60/$60–80   *"Art silk"' cardigan*

▼Another manufactured "art silk" cardigan, this time accompanied by an "art silk" blouse. Buttons on the cardigan were added later – it would originally have been worn with the cuffs turned back – and the colour combination of orange, cream, and grey is unusual. The blouse has machine embroidery and is very interesting for its wide asymmetrical collar. Looser necklines were popular as they flattened the bust and thus enhanced the boyish look.

"Art silk" cardigan

£80–120/$120–180

£50–70/$80–120

"Art silk" blouse

◄ This printed silk blouse is in the classic shade of orange popular in the inter-war years, known as "Tango". The ends of the scarf-tie form spear points, and separate spear scarves were also often worn with blouses in this period. The blouse falls in a straight line to hip level, where the resulting low waist is stressed by the horizontal bands.

£50–80/$80–120   *Orange blouse*

➤ This is a classic, clearly inspired by the *Ballets Russes*. Serge Diaghilev (1872–1929) and his company toured Europe before World War I, helping to popularize the fluid designs and vibrant colours of the set and costume designer Leon Bakst (1866–1924). A Cossack-style silk blouse, it has machine-embroidered sleeves and cuffs, and fastens with pearlized buttons.

Blouse   **£60–90/$80–120**

◄ The silk print of this vibrant dress is reminiscent of the work of textile designers such as Sonia Delaunay (1884–1979), who once had her car painted to match one of her most colourful dresses. Silk dresses like this need special care. The techniques used at the time mean that silk from the 1920s is very unstable today and therefore silk dresses are likely to fall apart if dry cleaned, washed, or hung in a wardrobe – they should be stored flat between layers of acid-free tissue paper.

Silk print dress   **£100–150/$150–200**

➤ The central panel in the bodice of this dress is reminiscent of the stomachers worn by women in the 18th century – many dresses of the 1920s adopted this style. The central panels were sometimes detachable, but this one is fixed to the bodice. The garment's trimmings are in a material of the same style and colour as the main dress, with the added rose print.

£150–200/$220–280 *"Art silk" jersey dress*

◄ This is 1920s fashion at its peak. You can imagine the wearer with her cloche pulled down low over her eyes, a cigarette glowing in its long holder, the picture of streamlined sophistication. This is a warm winter coat in fine wool, fastening at the hip with a single, black, self-covered button. The asymmetrical fur trimmings, the cut-out sections on the lower sleeves, and the stand-up collar all add to its value.

£300–400/$450–550 *Wool coat*

➤ Another example of the stylized flowers and exuberant colours of 1920s textiles (see p.33). This jacket is also in an artificial silk print, and is tailored so that the floral borders fall in all the right places – including the off-centre tie. Inside, the taffeta lining has a single deep pocket, and ties to ensure that it hangs properly. The jacket fastens with a single, self-covered button. Such buttons can often prove a nightmare for the collector as they are impossible to replace if lost.

"Art silk" jacket **£400–500/$600–800**

↑ This home-made silk dress is more subdued, and has a full skirt and puff sleeves. Despite its apparent simplicity, the piping and decoration at the hemline required skill. Home dressmaking was enormously popular during this time, partly because of the increased availability of home sewing machines. Many women widowed during World War I had families to support, and took to dressmaking as a practical way of earning a living.

Silk dress   **£150–200/$220–280**

↗ More 1920s exuberance. The upper two dresses, which belonged to a titled lady of the time, both make clever use of the centre panel. The pleats in the green silk dress on the left are in the same material as its centre panel. The black taffeta centre and hemline trimmings on the red, black, and white dress below were probably added later. Such alterations, common both during the 1930s as the Depression forced economies, and during the 1940s because of wartime shortages, detract from the value.

£50–80/$80–120   *Green dress (with damaged neckline)*

Green and orange dress   **£100–150/$150–200**

£60–90/$80–120   *Red, black, and white dress*

Eveningwear

For those with money, the high life in the 1920s could be tremendous fun – fancy-dress parties, scavenger hunts, night clubs, theatres and cinemas were among the diversions on offer. "Bright Young Things" drank cocktails, smoked, and further scandalized with their sexual ambivalence and their taste for cocaine and popular music, especially Jazz. Hemlines in eveningwear followed those for the daytime, remaining at ankle or calf length up to the mid-1920s, then becoming shorter until 1929, when collections featured hemlines lower at the back than the front. Throughout the decade, eveningwear still also meant floor-length dresses, especially slinky designs, which were worn alongside the shorter dresses essential for energetic dancers. Dancing was a popular obsession: the Charleston, the Blackbottom, and the Kickaboo ruled the floors at various times.

The fashion most readily associated with the 1920s is the beaded dress, and the bright, contrasting colours add to the appeal and value of this example. Beadwork and sequins need special care and attention on older dresses: thread weakens with age until the weight of the beads is too much for the dress, and special colours are very difficult to replace. These dresses are highly prized and widely sought after, but careful preservation over the years has ensured that a surprising number survive – perhaps because they could not be cut down for children's clothes and were no good for blacking out windows during World War II! Whatever the reason, dresses such as this one command the highest prices, especially when, as at present, current fashions echo their style.

£1800–2200/$2700–3200 *Beaded dress*

Another evening coat in immaculate condition, the devoré jacket with fringing has a Japanese design in velvet and is chiffon-lined. The skull-cap with net and gold sequins is typical of the vamp style popularized by the silent film actress Pola Negri. These caps were inspired by the Far East and remained in fashion well into the 1930s.

£300–400/$450–550 *Skull-cap*

£1700–2200/$2500–3500 *Jacket*

◄ This coat, with its wonderful expansive fur collar, has a single hip-button fastening, popular in the 1920s. Once again, it is in a rich, metallic-threaded cloth with a floral-based pattern. Fashionable 1920s women would hold clutch bags, their arms heavy with bracelets worn in multiples on each arm. Society heiress Nancy Cunard encouraged this trend, and was photographed by Cecil Beaton with her arms covered in African bangles in a celebrated portrait which epitomizes the period.

Evening coat   **£700–1000/$1000–1500**

◄ A characteristic 1920s dress and bolero. The panels of the skirt overlap around the dress, allowing more freedom to show directoire knickers. The panels also pad out the hips, reminiscent of the panniers popular on dresses around World War I. The bolero has metal slugs sewn round its waist to ensure it hangs properly, making the outfit surprisingly heavy.

£400–400/$600–800

Jacket and bolero

◄ This knee-length coat could be worn over a dress of any length. The full ruched collar is very 1920s. Eveningwear is often easier to find today than daywear, as evening garments were worn only on special occasions. This coat is a prime example – the metallic threads are in very good condition – and should command a high price because of the collectability of high 1920s style and also the richness of both fabric and design.

£600–800/$900–1100   *Opera cloak*

Lingerie

Boned and padded corsets were conspicuous by their absence from the 1920s right up until the late 1940s. Part of this was the influence of Paul Poiret, whose "hobble" skirts had freed women from the constraints imposed by the ideal of the "S" silhouette. Another factor was new technology – corsetry of the 1920s relied on woven elastic materials rather than whalebone and padding. But perhaps the major influence was the fashion for androgyny rather than femininity after World War I – underwear played its part by flattening curves and compressing the buttocks and the bust. This tubular shape continued to be popular, with minor variations, throughout the 1920s. Camiknickers, combining the camisole and knickers, were a new fashion at the start of the decade. Known as "step-ins" after the method of putting them on, they were part of a trend towards wearing fewer, and less constricting, undergarments. Initially, ivory was the most popular colour for lingerie, but pink and peach also took their turn. In the late 1920s the word "bra", short for brassière, came into use, and different cup sizes were introduced.

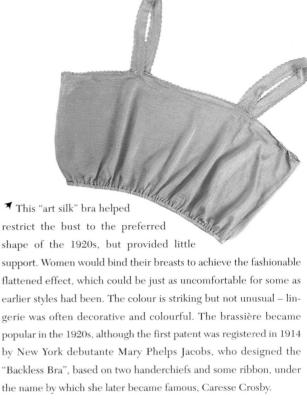

↖ This "art silk" bra helped restrict the bust to the preferred shape of the 1920s, but provided little support. Women would bind their breasts to achieve the fashionable flattened effect, which could be just as uncomfortable for some as earlier styles had been. The colour is striking but not unusual – lingerie was often decorative and colourful. The brassière became popular in the 1920s, although the first patent was registered in 1914 by New York debutante Mary Phelps Jacobs, who designed the "Backless Bra", based on two handerchiefs and some ribbon, under the name by which she later became famous, Caresse Crosby.

Brassière   **£50–80/$80–120**

↘ Garters from the 1920s are rare these days, but were essential to the wardrobe. The top pair is in printed ribbon, and the lower pair in elasticated satin with sequin decorations – metal garters were also popular. At strategic moments women had to adjust their garters to avoid cutting off the circulation to the legs. Jazz pianist Lil Hardin recalled how other (male) members of King Oliver's Band would take particular interest as she adjusted her garters to sit at the piano.

£60–80/$100–150
Garters with floral decoration

£50–70/$70–90
Yellow satin garters

◄ Knees were now visible to the world at large, so stockings that flattered the legs were popular, and were soon freely available in an enormous range of styles and colours, as production increased to take advantage of the newly expanding market. This beautiful pair of artificial silk stockings is machine-embroidered. It was quite the thing to show the tops of one's stockings – which is why, like many stockings of the period, these are quite short and have contrasting stitching at the tops.

£60–80/$90–120   *Purple art silk stockings*

➤ "Directoire" knickers were essential for those who enjoyed the new energetic, high-kicking dances like the Charleston and the Blackbottom. This pair, in silk with machine embroidery, is quite voluminous. The name was taken from the pantaloons of a similar style worn by fashionable French ladies during the rule of the Directory in Paris at the end of the 18th century. However smaller French knickers were more popular by the end of the 1920s.

"Directoire" knickers   **£60–90/$90–120**

*"Roll 'em high or low just as you please,
Don't let people tell you that it's shocking,
Paint your sweetie's picture on your stocking"*

from *Roll 'em Girls (roll your own)*,
a popular song of the 1920s

◄ This is the "Dracolena" corset or vestette, generically known as a combinaire. It is made from artificial silk jersey, with elastic suspenders for the stockings – the colour is "Tea Rose". It is more valuable because it comes in its original box and is unworn, so the elastic remains in perfect condition. This all-in-one style of garment is clearly designed to flatten curves and would have been worn along with separate knickers.

Combinaire in original box   **£80–120/$120–180**

Accessories

Accessories from the 1920s, as those of any other era, tell us a great deal about the social interests and preoccupations of the decade. The discovery by Howard Carter of the tomb of the Egyptian pharaoh Tutankhamun, in 1922, caught everyone's imagination, and Egyptian-style accessories were soon all the rage. Women could buff their nails on "Egyptien Nail Polishing Stone" (*sic*) and keep sunburst-decorated "flapjacks" (small powder compacts) in their Egyptian-style handbags. The use of cosmetics became increasingly daring, and traditionalists were shocked when "Bright Young Things" applied rouge in public. However, the practice was commonplace, as is reflected by the built-in mirrors in handbags from the 1920s onwards. Vintage handbags are extremely collectable today, being easy to store, good to mix and match, and still very practical. However, prices reflect their collectability. Less popular among collectors are shoes, which are more difficult to find in the correct sizes – feet in the 1920s were in general much smaller than feet today. Hats are very collectable, being eminently wearable and often still in good condition. Lovers of slim lines should look out for the typical 1920s bell-shaped cloche.

The smart 1920s woman matched colours on hats, bags, shoes, and dresses, but the owner of this printed silk bag and scarf went one step further by fully co-ordinating her accessories. Both the large, stylized flowers, and the bright, contrasting colours are typical of the period, as is the asymmetrical flap on the bag.

Scarf and handbag   **£200–300/$300–400**

In the daytime, a woman might wear this leather peep-toe pair of shoes made by Dr Scholl's, a concern established in 1904 by a Chicago doctor who decided to specialize in footwear. Famed for its wooden-soled, leather flip-flops, which unexpectedly became fashion items in the 1960s, the firm is still in existence today. This pair of shoes is complete with its original matching laces, which will add to the value. Vintage shoes are not especially popular with collectors, as they can be difficult to display, are susceptible to damage, and are often hard to find in the right size.

Shoes   **£120–180/$180–220**

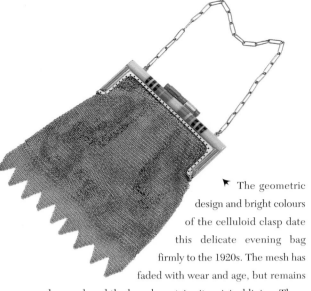

⌐ The geometric design and bright colours of the celluloid clasp date this delicate evening bag firmly to the 1920s. The mesh has faded with wear and age, but remains undamaged, and the bag also retains its original lining. These factors make the bag very collectable today. Before buying any vintage bag, always remember to check inside it!

Evening bag   **£150–200/$200–300**

⌐ Tutankhamun was the inspiration for this red-leather handbag – a connection that significantly increases its value to the collector. It is decorated with machine-stitched embroidery, gilt "wings", and a "scarab" stud fastening made of Bakelite. The silk lining is divided into three compartments, one of which has a built-in mirror for checking make-up. The bag would have held a brightly printed "art silk" handkerchief, powder, a rouge compact, a lip colour, and, if you were really daring, cigarettes.

Egyptian-style handbag   **£250–350/$400–500**

⌐ The cloche originates from around 1924, when it perfectly complemented short hair cut in the new bobbed or cropped styles. Cloches were worn fitted as close to the head as possible, pulled down low so that the eyes were barely visible. They did not require hat pins to stay in place, and were therefore perfect for wearing while motoring, or, for the very upmarket, while flying in aeroplanes. This version, in a typical 1920s "Tango" orange, is decorated with exotic feathers – a fashion that by the 1930s had seriously reduced wild bird populations. The black hat, which is covered in intricate hand embroidery, is French. Cloches are very collectable, and also extremely wearable. Prices vary enormously and depend on the styling and condition. Sometimes linings have been damaged or removed, and this too affects the value.

"Tango" orange cloche   **£300–400/$450–550**

Black hand-decorated cloche   **£350–450/$500–600**

Menswear

Men in the 1920s had some challenging icons: the Prince of Wales, Rudolph Valentino, and Douglas Fairbanks all influenced styles in dress. In the immediate post-war period the first hesitant steps were taken towards greater informality. Only elderly gentlemen now wore frock coats away from the most formal occasions, and soft collars became commonplace on shirts. Fair Isle pullovers, wide lapels, brogues, and trousers with belts were a few of the innovations sparked by the Prince of Wales. Hats were still worn by men of all classes: the well-heeled would have a bowler for work, a formal top hat, a cap for sportswear, and a soft felt hat for the country. Wool was everywhere, although louche men-about-town such as Noel Coward were photographed in their silk dressing gowns and cravats. In this decade Oxford University and its predominantly male undergraduates wielded significant sartorial influence, popularizing styles in brogues, striped blazers, and the wide trousers called "Oxford bags".

◄ In the 1920s a wool cloak with satin lining and brocade fastening such as this would be worn to the opera or theatre, accompanied by a top hat and a silver-topped cane. Men's formal wear changed little at the beginning of the 1920s – these were times when men wore clothes rather than the year's fashions, so there was little impetus for change. Linings are always important for the collector – damaged or torn ones are often removed, and this detracts from a garment's value.

Cloak   **£180–220/$250–350**

▼ An example of growing informality in hats, this is a Panama-style example, made in Italy. The Panama hat came from Ecuador and was introduced to Europe by Napoleon III in 1855. Trimmed with black silk ribbons, many examples have the name "Panama" in the headbands. Boaters were also popular hats for men at leisure. Originally from Paris, boaters were first worn by rowers in the 1870s, thus acquiring their name.

Panama   **£45–55/$70–90**

➤ Knickerbockers had been worn for golf for some time, but plus fours, introduced in the 1920s, were another of the Prince of Wales's innovations. They owed their name to the additional material used in their design: the extra four inches, falling initially below the knee, were gathered to give maximum room and comfort. This pair, in rough wool, is a mixture of pale blue, dark brown, and yellow threads. The pockets are enormous, perfect for holding golf balls, and the leather strap at each knee gathers the loose material together with a double-pronged buckle.

Plus fours   **£180–220/$270–350**

◀ Motoring was still the pastime of the well-off in the 1920s. The unheated and frequently open-topped cars of the time required special clothing. This coat is in thick leather and would have been worn with a close-fitting helmet and goggles. Cars often broke down, so a journey of any length would probably involve time spent tinkering with the recalcitrant engine. This was commemorated in a popular song of the time: "He had to get under, get out and get under, to fix up his automobile."

£300–400/$450–580   *Car coat*

➤ These white, Egyptian-cotton trousers are typical of the 1920s with their wide cut, high waist, and generous crotch. They have button fastening on the fly, and buttons around the waistband to fix braces. Sportswear, especially cricket flannels and jumpers, is often associated with the 1920s, and these trousers show the authentic shape and style of the period. Their value is enhanced because they are in Egyptian cotton, the best quality cotton available.

Cotton trousers   **£250–350/$400–500**

The Thirties

The Wall Street Crash of 1929 marked the end of a carefree decade in America and the start of a cashless one. During the 1930s a much softer, feminine look replaced the sleek and boyish shape of the 1920s. Skirts fell, initially to mid-calf, and a soft line from shoulder to waist was an enduring theme. Sophistication was the keynote: women wanted to look alluring, and by the late 1930s romanticism had taken over. New developments in printing and photography encouraged the glamorous portrait photography of Dorothy Wilding and Cecil Beaton. Tennis, cycling, and motoring were increasingly popular pastimes — showing a tan and dieting were soon essential for the sporting silhouette. Women now wore close-fitting wool swimming costumes and spent their holidays at the seaside. The Russian artist Cassandre captured the new obsession with speed and streamlining in his advertising posters. Glamorous journeys on liners such as the Queen Mary were beyond most people, but trains went faster for everyone. The Depression eased as the 1930s went on, to be replaced by fears of war which finally became a reality in September 1939.

Daywear

Coco Chanel and Jean Patou set the trend for sartorial sophistication for the next decade when, in 1929, their autumn collections featured a soft curving line from the shoulder to a high waist. Almost overnight, the flappers and the Jazz Babies were out of date. The boyish look of the "Roaring Twenties" was replaced by a new, feminine style that was initially subtle, alluring, and sophisticated. By the time war broke out, at the end of 1939, it had become highly romantic and broadly retrospective. People did not immediately stop wearing the styles of the 1920s in favour of the new shapes, but by the mid-1930s the influence of film stars such as Claudette Colbert and Marlene Dietrich held sway, and many, including Jean Harlow, modelled for the Paris fashion houses. The theme of the sporty woman was boosted during the 1930s by another actress, Katherine Hepburn. The daughter of a well-to-do American family, she regularly dressed in men's clothes and popularized wide, practical trousers. Her approach was probably the first major anti-fashion statement.

◄ These linen trousers are by Lillywhites, the British sportswear company, and are elegant and slimming to wear, having a generous cut. They fasten with a side zipper, which remained the style in women's trousers until the arrival of the Unisex movement in the late 1960s. Zip fasteners usually had metal teeth before World War II, but as early as 1935 Elsa Schiaparelli (1890–1973) used fasteners with plastic teeth in her annual collection.

Linen trousers   **£70–100/$100–150**

▼ Lounging pyjamas became popular during the 1920s, having evolved from the craze for trousers which began when women dressed for factory work during World War I. A "Bright Young Thing" would own different types for wearing around the house in the daytime, for eveningwear, and for the beach. This pair is in lemon and black silk, and so would have been rather impractical as beachwear, but perfect for relaxing at home.

£120–180/$180–220

Silk lounging pyjamas

◄ A 1930s masterpiece, this coat and dress set is hand-finished. All the seams are matched to emphasize the geometry of the fabric, a heavy crêpe jersey which must have been incredibly difficult to sew. The cape, stitched directly to the coat, has pin tucks and pleats. The survival of the asymmetrical Bakelite coat fastening and original dress belt add to the value.

£700–1000/$1000–1500 *Coat and dress set*

▼ Kick pleats in contrasting materials were often used in the centres or sides of skirts during the 1920s and 30s. The asymmetrically placed button and the longer length put this dress firmly in the mid-1930s. It is in crêpe and, typically, fastens at the side and at the cuffs with hooks and eyes.

Dress   **£70–100/$100–150**

► Fairly simple in both design and cut, this dress and coat are in black crêpe and printed silk. Despite the relaxation of social conventions, a certain formality in women's wear remained – dress and coat ensembles such as this would be worn on special occasions. Appliqué was a popular form of decorating, and here the floral panel on the dress has simply been cut out of a length of printed silk and stitched roughly onto it.

£250–300/$350–450 *Dress and coat set*

➤ Another coat and dress ensemble: the coat (not shown) is in brown velvet, lined with the brown and white satin from which the bodice of this romantic dress is also made. Despite their flowing appearance, the sleeves are very narrow by today's standards. Clothes from the 1920s are often very small – the average person today is much taller and far larger framed than his or her early 20th-century counterpart.

Dress (with matching coat not shown) **£450–550/$600–800**

➤ Very feminine in style and material, this satin print blouse has a high waist and toning plastic buttons. New techniques and materials, particularly Bakelite and later plastics, make buttons of this period worth collecting for themselves, with examples available in combinations of metal, plastic, glass, and wood. Also common on 1930s buttons were bright colours and appropriate pictorial designs, such as stylized golfers for use on golfing outfits.

Blouse **£60–90/$90–120**

➤ Jazzy prints were in demand throughout the 1930s, but this skirt is interesting both for the shade of green and the style of its flowers. Apple green was to the 1930s what aubergine was to the 1970s – it was used everywhere in fabrics and furnishings. The flowers are much simpler than in 1920s designs – this softer approach sums up the difference in style between the two decades.

Skirt **£50–80/$80–120**

◄ Another classic. The free-flowing lines and stark simplicity of this suit show just how far the influence of Coco Chanel reached. The pockets on the tunic are purely decorative and just right for a couple of artificial silk handkerchiefs. A belt, which would have been in the same olive-green material, is missing from the top. The smart 1930s woman would have matched the colour of the dark brown collar with her gloves, hat, handbag, and shoes. Kick pleats around the hem of the skirt add to the fluidity of the garment.

Suit **£180–220/$250–350**

➤ Another example of subdued colouring and simple design. The Wall Street Crash of 1929 and the subsequent depression during the 1930s encouraged a more sombre approach to daywear. Following the death of George V in 1935, black, to symbolize mourning, was the only possible colour for fashion leaders in the UK. The anticipated coronation of Edward VIII, the playboy Prince of Wales, encouraged a more colourful turn, which his subsequent abdication did little to dispel.

£80–120/$120–180 *Blouse*

◄ Abstract paintings were popular in Russia and Italy during the 1930s, but in much of Europe, and in the USA, abstract patterns were more often used in design, including textiles. This cardigan has had some amendments: its cuffs and banding have been replaced, and the buttons are later additions. The collector of vintage tops should be aware that some knitted garments from the 1920s were cut down to suit the new, shorter 1930s lengths.

£100–150/$150–200 *Cardigan*

Eveningwear

Floor-length eveningwear was the style in the 1930s, following the demise of the flapper and her straight-line, knee-length dresses. Women wore clinging, backless gowns or period, revival-style designs ranging from Grecian and Medieval Romantic, through the wasp-waists and bustles of the 19th century, to ultra-modern designs with wide, padded shoulders. In 1933 *Vogue's* diary went to a party given by the designer Syrie Maugham (1879–1955), and related how "Beatrice Lillie holds up the skirt of her light but long sealing-wax silk dress, in the refined manner of 1898 ... [and] ... Tilly Losch has just arrived from her ballet in white with green polka dots" – an accurate reflection of the eclectic mix of styles in 1930s fashion. In the USA the end of Prohibition did nothing to diminish the popularity of wining and dining the night away in clubs. On both sides of the Atlantic the "Smart Set" drank cocktails and danced to the bands of Artie Shaw, Benny Goodman, and Nat Gonella – and whatever the individual style worn, the aim was sophistication.

➤ Clothes made of velvet, such as this chocolate-brown jacket and evening hat, were popular during the 1930s. Ostrich feathers, which decorate the hat above, were also still fashionable. The collar of this delicate jacket extends to an asymmetrical scarf tie. It is in devoré, a collectable, and often highly priced, figured velvet, and in this example the fabric is sculpted in an attractive leaf pattern.

Hat **£100–150/$150–200** *Jacket* **£800–1000/$1200–1800**

◄ As the decade progressed, outright romanticism became increasingly fashionable. One women's magazine advised readers to update an evening dress that was "too austere" by sewing silk lampshade fringe a shade darker than the gown around its neckline. This dress, in printed silk chiffon, has feminine frills at the sleeves, and to emphasize the train. The small cut-outs at the front echo dramatic cut-out panels running from shoulder to waistline at the back.

Dress **£800–1200/$1200–1800**

This lined, satin-print evening jacket is a classic 1930s design. Both the short length and the shape of the collar emphasize the soft lines and the high waist of the typical silhouette of the time. The colours too – especially the jade green – are characteristic of the period, and the tulip was a very popular motif.

Jacket **£500–600/$750–850**

← Fashion designer Jasper Conran (b.1959) remarked that bias-cutting is vicious, and this is about as vicious as you can get: a beautiful evening dress, with a multi-coloured top emphasizing the line of the shoulders and bust, while the belted skirt stresses the shape and size of the hips – whatever that may be. The wearer would have felt fabulous wearing this dress, provided that she stood up straight and didn't eat a thing.

£350–450/$500–600

Dress

↑ This bias-cut, gold-lamé evening dress, with matching jacket, has a low-cut back and is soft and clinging. The enormous popularity of bias-cutting at this time sparked the production of many close-fitting dresses that flowed in flattering folds around the hem. This example is missing its original belt, which reduces the value. Most dresses of this period had simple belts, usually in the same material. The shoes, by Coles of Sheffield, are in black silk and gold leather, and are reminiscent of the ubiquitous Art Deco sunburst motif of the 1920s and 30s.

Dress/jacket **£700–1000/$1000–1500**   *Shoes* **£250–350/$350–450**

Lingerie

The suspender belt was a 1930s innovation, and, as stockings became longer, stocking tops were definitely not for show. Here, as everywhere else at this time, the aristocracy earned extra cash through endorsements: the Duchess of Kent lent her name to Embassy stockings (pure silk and far from cheap!). As hemlines dropped, stockings became more subdued in tone – variations in shades of brown were soon the most common. Stockings came in combinations of silk, "art silk", and Lisle, a two-ply twisted cotton yarn. Bias-cut dresses made it vital that underwear appeared to be seamfree. The silhouettes of the early 1930s were defined by underwear that encouraged free movement – rather than being imprisoned in whalebone stays, women were gently moulded into the preferred shape by elastic and rubber foundation garments. It was even rumoured that, in order to perfect her much admired silhouette, actress Jean Harlow wore no lingerie at all. As the 1940s loomed, however, the fashion for a more exaggerated form demanded underwear that sculpted the wearer to achieve a small waist and generous bosom. The popularity of Victorian and Edwardian shapes resulted in the return of the bustle and corset, although new versions took advantage of flexible, lightweight fabrics and plastic boning.

➤ Pale pink and fastened with a button, this artificial silk bra has no elastic at all, and so can only be adjusted be removing and replacing the button. The cups are shaped by strategically placed darts.

Bra   **£35–45/$50–80**

◄ These French knickers, known as "Mother Trusts Me" according to underwear collector Rosemary Hawthorne, are, like the bra above, in silk façonné, the term for fabrics in which motifs are woven into the cloth. French knickers remained popular until the 1950s.

£30–40/$45–55   *French knickers*

◄ These silk stockings are in the shade known as "Coppertint". Bondor was a well-known brand, and later merged with Kayser. Women would often buy such stockings from door-to-door salesmen. They were sold in Cellophane wrapping or in boxes, and manufacturers attached small cards of the same wool or silk for darning. Pairs with labels or wool cards still attached, or in their original boxes, fetch higher prices.

Stockings in box   **£30–40/$45–55**

◄ Black underwear from the 1930s is very rare, and this silk and lace set was made to measure. Women often made their own underwear from paper patterns, or knitted items from two-ply wool, but these camiknickers were made in Britain by Kayser, a company that still manufactures lingerie today. Central heating was far from universal in homes, so warm underwear was essential in the winter. Camiknickers such as the pink set here were especially suitable under bias-cut dresses as they had no seams to spoil the line of the outer garment.

Black camiknickers **£100–150/$150–200**
Pink camiknickers **£60–80/$90–120**

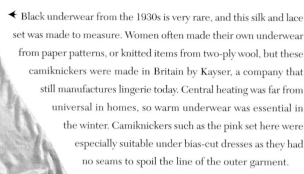

▼ ◄ The green slip below on the right is another example of home-made underwear. Patterns were regularly given away free with women's magazines. The blue rayon jersey slip is hand-finished and made by Palmers, a company which, like Kayser, still produces lingerie today. This slip includes all its original labels, which adds to the value. One label includes detailed instructions in German advising that it should be washed "similar to wool articles".

£70–£100/$100–150 *Blue slip with labels*

Green slip **£40–50/$60–80**

▲ The loose cut and the side-button fastening indicate that these pyjamas, made from artificial silk jersey, were definitely for wearing in the bedroom. Pyjamas first originated in India, as did their name – women did not begin wearing them in bed until the 1920s.

Pyjamas **£100–150/$150–200**

Accessories

Everything must be chosen and matched with care – that was the order for accessories in the 1930s. Women would change shoes, bags, hats, and scarves as they changed their clothes during the day. Handbags often had built-in mirrors, matching purses, and pockets for combs, innovations which did not go down well with everyone. "The majority of men like bobbed hair," claimed *Good Housekeeping* in 1931, "but no man can abide the contemporary habit of combing the hair in public, especially at a dinner table, nor does any man like to see a woman lipsticking herself in public." The parasol, an essential feature in previous decades, was now optional as the fashion for a golden tan caught hold. Fur stoles were vital fashion accessories in the early years of the decade, but, as the Depression dragged on, their popularity waned – in 1937 the advice was "If you must wear fur, dye it." Hats were a riot of shapes and styles. The cloche style was too convenient to fade away quickly, but soon women were also wearing large picture hats, tall, angular ones, and more masculine "slouch" styles in tweed. The original slouch hat was created for Greta Garbo by Adrian (1903–59).

◄ The 1939 World's Fair, held in New York, celebrated all the achievements of the early 20th Century. As with the 1925 Fair in France, which defined Art Deco style, countries from across the world exhibited the latest designs in New York. Fashion was represented in the Textile Building, and numerous commemorative items were available at the Fair. Scarves which mark important events are much sought after by collectors.

Scarf **£40–50/$60–80**

▼ Handbags in the 1930s were often plain and followed simple, geometric shapes. The one on the left is in blue leather on a chrome frame and has a built-in mirror and an integral purse. The black leather handbag has a handle of Bakelite, a material invented in 1907 by Belgian chemist Leo Hendrik Baekeland – the first entirely synthetic plastic. Silk and rayon handkerchiefs are still easy to find and match with outfits.

£200–300/$300–400 *Chrome handbag*

Handkerchief **£10–15/$15–20**

£80–120/$120–180 *Bakelite handbag*

⌄ These two hats sum up the diversity of styles in the 1930s. The velvet turban was made popular by the actress Joan Crawford. The suede leather hat has a Harrods label, and its lone spear of leather mimics designs in felt with single feathers. Probably the most famous hat of the time was the Shoe Hat by Elsa Schiaparelli. Designed in collaboration with the Surrealist Salvador Dali, it was shaped like an upturned shoe, complete with a heel in Schiaparelli's trademark colour, shocking pink.

£80–120/$120–180 *Red turban*

£100–150/$150–200 *Harrods hat*

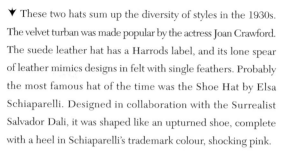

⌃ One solution to the difficulty of matching accessories was to make them from the same material. By the late 1930s, small waists and full skirts were emphasized by coloured belts, anticipating the New Look of 1947. This scarf and belt set is in fine wool with a metallic thread in a zig-zag pattern, but the buckle on the leather-lined belt is not original.

Scarf and belt **£70–100/$100–150**

↤ Gauntlets were mainly for town or smarter wear, but these are obviously designed with driving in mind. Women wore gloves on both formal and informal occasions, which were often highly decorated with embroidery or contrasting panels, and could be worn long. Women also sported softer, short gloves in wool and cloth with their country outfits.

£50–80/$80–120 *Gauntlets*

55

Menswear

Men, like women, adopted a more subtle, languid approach to their clothes in the 1930s. Hollywood favoured action men like Clark Gable. Manufacturers of underwear breathed a collective sigh of relief when, in the 1934 film *It Happened One Night*, Gable took off his shirt to reveal that, contrary to popular myth, real men wore vests. Underpants were not commonplace: a population survey in Britain during World War II confirmed that men owned on average only one pair of pants – so quite a few men probably wore none at all. Corduroy trousers and suede shoes, initially seen as the affectation of artists and other Bohemians, became immensely popular with men of all backgrounds. The dinner jacket, or tuxedo, was the preferred style for eveningwear, and Fred Astaire made it the epitome of evening elegance in his films with Ginger Rogers, although he sometimes sported full evening dress too. Tuxedos took their name from the Tuxedo Club in America and were double-breasted between the wars.

◄ A typical jacket from the late 1930s – it has four, rather than six, buttons. The wide weave of this jacket sums up the studied and casual approach that was increasingly dominant in the decade's menswear. This example was styled by Bakers of Golden Square, in the West End of London, a fashionable address at the time.

£120–180/$180–220

White jacket

▼ Another royal influence, the homburg was first introduced by Edward VII, grandfather of the Prince of Wales (who temporarily became Edward VIII in the course of 1936). In the 1930s the homburg was so closely associated with the dapper British foreign secretary, Anthony Eden, that hatters put pictures of him, suitably attired, in their windows. When he resigned in 1938 over his government's appeasement of Hitler at Munich, the homburg was declared passé and the bowler adopted as its successor.

Homburg   **£80–120/$120–180**

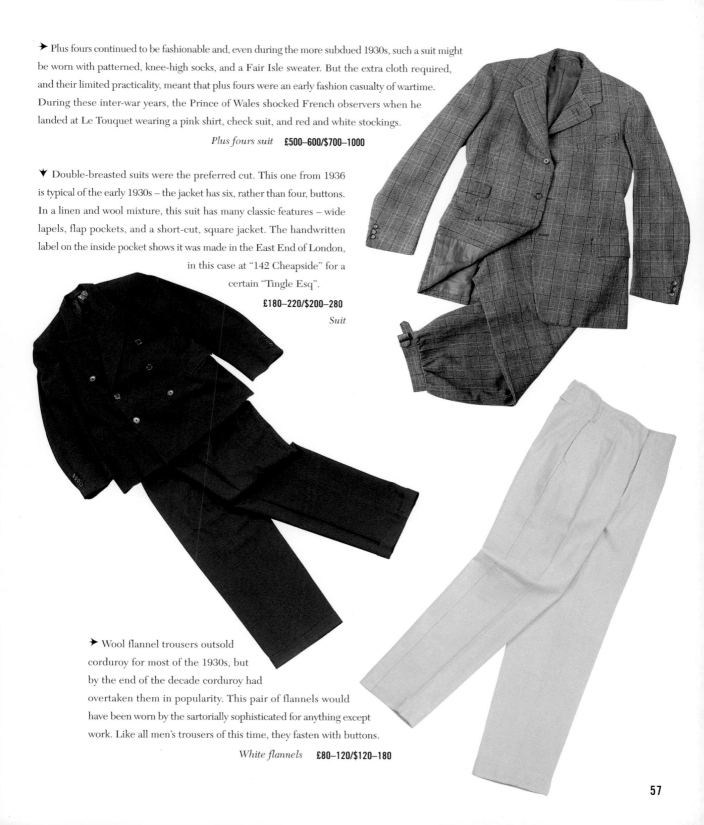

➤ Plus fours continued to be fashionable and, even during the more subdued 1930s, such a suit might be worn with patterned, knee-high socks, and a Fair Isle sweater. But the extra cloth required, and their limited practicality, meant that plus fours were an early fashion casualty of wartime. During these inter-war years, the Prince of Wales shocked French observers when he landed at Le Touquet wearing a pink shirt, check suit, and red and white stockings.

Plus fours suit **£500–600/$700–1000**

▼ Double-breasted suits were the preferred cut. This one from 1936 is typical of the early 1930s – the jacket has six, rather than four, buttons. In a linen and wool mixture, this suit has many classic features – wide lapels, flap pockets, and a short-cut, square jacket. The handwritten label on the inside pocket shows it was made in the East End of London, in this case at "142 Cheapside" for a certain "Tingle Esq".

£180–220/$200–280

Suit

➤ Wool flannel trousers outsold corduroy for most of the 1930s, but by the end of the decade corduroy had overtaken them in popularity. This pair of flannels would have been worn by the sartorially sophisticated for anything except work. Like all men's trousers of this time, they fasten with buttons.

White flannels **£80–120/$120–180**

57

The Forties

Wartime shortages in Britain led to the creation of Utility clothing. This strict code took a practical approach to using less fabric, and fewer trimmings and fastenings, and set the sartorial tone for the war years. Under its famous trademark "CC41" ("CC" for Civilian Clothing, "41" for the year Utility was introduced) it was soon applied to other goods, and a similar scheme was set up in America under the L-85 regulations. In the post-war years shortages worsened, and when Christian Dior unveiled his "New Look" in 1947, the extravagance of his dresses provoked fury in Paris. Picking up where the the hour-glass figure of the late 1930s had left off, Dior used yards of material, bringing back the wasp waist, the curved bust, high heels, and abundant ornamentation. Fellow designer Cristobal Balenciaga, while fastening a 30-button Dior dress on a client, exclaimed "Christian is mad, mad!" An American customer wrote to Dior that he had "disfigured my wife with your genius. I want to make you a proposition. Why don't I send you the remains? She is about a size 46." Utility continued in production until 1951, but, after enduring all the restrictions of wartime, everyone wanted the Dior look.

Daywear

Shortages of material meant that women had little need of encouragement from the Board of Trade to "Go through Your Wardrobe and Make Do and Mend". As in World War I, trousers were more common apparel for women. But women now wore boiler suits too, called "Siren Suits" because they were easy to pull on when a siren warning of an air-raid was heard. Designers threw themselves into the war effort: Digby Morton (1906–83) did most to popularize the tailored suit, and also designed the Women's Voluntary Service uniform. Suits with sharp shoulders and skirts which finished around the knee, worn for work, socializing, and weddings, were chic reactions to the restrictions. Hair was worn off the face, and was kept short or tied back, as war work in factories and farms meant that long hair could catch in machinery. After the war, the impact of Dior's "New Look", given its name by Carmel Snow, the celebrated editor of *Vogue* and fashion editor of *Harper's Bazaar,* began to be felt. Dior himself called it the "Corolle" line, because of the huge skirts which spread, like a flower's corolla of petals, from a tiny waistline.

This post-war dress, with its decorative quilting and fancy buttons, is a variation of the "shirt-waister" style, a practical but stylish design which has stayed around the borders of fashion ever since. The linen and cotton mixture is hard-wearing, and the combination of fabrics means that it moves easily but does not crease. The most successful linen mixture was sold under the trademark Moygashel.

Yellow dress   £100–150/$150–200

A linen Utility dress with its original plain buckled belt and flocking stencil motif. The Utility scheme limited designers in Britain with such rules as a maximum of three buttons to a jacket, and banned heels more than two inches high, peep toes, turned-back cuffs and button-down pockets. It was applied to bags, shoes, and underwear, wherever raw or recycled materials could be saved. Bias-cutting was certainly out of the question.

£120–180/$180–220

Poodle dress

◄ This blouse, also Utility, comes from the British retail chain Marks & Spencer (est.1894). Utility clothes can seem more decorative than might be expected, as with these attractive buttons, but were plain by comparison with fashions of the 1930s. Some collectors specialize in Utility clothes which, being generally well made, remain in good condition and are reasonably priced.

Blouse   **£50–80/$80–120**

➤ Suits became popular in the 1940s, as they were practical and often, like this one, quite striking. The jackets were worn over plain blouses or hand-knitted jumpers in bright colours made from odds and ends of wool. During the war, women sometimes cut themselves suits from the evening clothes left by their absent husbands.

£120–180/$180-220   *Blue suit*

In these days of shortage — choose classics every time!

Fashion hint from *Picture Post*
February 1944

◄ Hand-knitting retained its popularity in the 1940s, but the range of wools was severely restricted – it was usual to reknit wool unpicked from old garments. Clever uses of various textures and thicknesses of wool often resulted, as in this sweater. Short sleeves were almost universal, and were sometimes puffed or pleated. The sloping shoulders and high waist were constant, but in the late 1940s tight sweaters, as worn by the film star Lana Turner (famous as "the Sweater Girl"), were all the rage.

Jumper   **£40–50/$60–80**

◄ The Women's Voluntary Service was founded by Lady Reading in 1938. A volunteer civilian force, it worked with other civil defence services during bombing raids and their aftermath. The only colour available for their uniform was green, already rejected by other civil services on superstitious grounds – to overcome this, the twill cloth was woven with green and grey wool. A warm and well-cut coat, this one was worn by a member in Surrey, and the badges increase the value, particularly as such items are also sought by civil defence collectors.

WVS overcoat   **£180–220/$220–280**

▼ Adapted forms of the extremes of the New Look did reach those women who did not buy haute couture. The gathered waist, full skirt, and longer lengths of Dior's original all filtered through to the High Street. Coats fell to mid-calf, about 25cm (10in) from the ground. Large buttons covered in crocodile skin add a touch of drama to this example. The buttonholes have been repaired. By the end of the 1940s, coats had lost the waist altogether as swing and tent shapes took over.

Brown coat   **£150–200/$180–220**

◄ A warm plaid coat by fashion retailers Alexon, with very distinctive painted wooden buttons. The cold weather in the later 1940s was so extreme that it set records, but heavy overcoats, fitted close to the body, still managed to be fashionable. The influence of military uniforms on design prompted the return of the greatcoat – a similar phenomenon occurred at the end of World War I.

Plaid coat   **£160–200/$240–280**

A mixture of tweed and other wool combines to ensure a hard-wearing suit. Its buttons and decorative pocket flaps show that it is definitely not Utility. This suit would not have been subject to the price controls which kept the cost of Utility items down, so would have been very expensive in both money and clothing coupons.

Suit   **£120–180/$180–220**

Swagger coats, known in the USA as toppers, flowed outwards from the shoulder. The length of the jacket varied, but the style became immensely popular in the 1950s. Full-length versions were known as swing and, later, tent coats. These two examples are both in wool with toning linings and buttons. The pink one is labelled "Tailored by Wesdo".

Swagger coats (each)   **£180–220/$220–280**

Eveningwear

While women in Britain were instructed to "Make Do and Mend", in the USA women were encouraged to buy clothes to support the war effort. However elegance was still craved on both sides of the Atlantic. After the liberation of Paris from Nazi occupation, the city suffered from the Allied wartime shortages but, as 1945 passed, eveningwear in particular tried to reflect a more luxurious style. In the post-war era, ballgowns, and stiff petticoats they required, brought their own problems which the wealthy at least could solve: it was said that when Baroness de Rothschild discovered that even her largest limousine would crush her dress, she went to a ball in a horse box. Full-length and knee-length dresses were both perfectly acceptable for eveningwear during the 1940s, but trousers remained less common despite their adoption as daywear.

◄ An immensely detailed dress in a linen-mixture fabric: the skirt has a fringed train at the back which hangs from under a pleated panel. The sleeves have cut-out shapes, and the overall effect is reminiscent of 1930s styles, many of which continued into the early 1940s. This dress is in excellent condition, including the fringe. The value will be affected if any strands of the fringe are missing, frayed, or tangled.

Long dress **£400–500/$600–750**

▼ This evening jacket is in richly textured velvet, and fastens with just a single large hook at the collar. The shape means it is clearly from the late 1940s, and the style remained popular throughout the next decade too. The brooch, dating from twenty years earlier, is in chrome with paste stones arranged in an Art Deco design. A nostalgia for the early 1920s sprang up in the late 1940s among people young enough not to remember them.

£180–220/$270–330
Swing jacket
£50–80/$80–120
Brooch

➤ This full-length dress has the central ruching so admired at the time, and is in a very heavy linen fabric. The ruched centre panel runs the full length of the torso from the neckline. The bag, made in England, is in a satin brocade. Accessories for eveningwear and, sometimes, daywear would include a bag in matching colours, long gloves, and, with full-length dresses especially, long ear-rings as well.

£150–200/$220–280   *Dress*

£60–80/$80–120   *Bag*

➤ A magnificent dress in gold lamé with panniers, ruching, gathers, and pleats, all of which demand a slender figure. During the 1940s the designer Charles James (1906–78) produced some of his finest "sculpted" dresses for his numerous wealthy clients. Often asymmetrical, they were padded and cut in order to achieve the desired shape.

£700–1000/$1000–1500   *Gold dress*

➤ This brocade taffeta dress would be worn with several layers of stiff petticoats to emphasize the scalloped edge. Three-quarter-length sleeves, as seen here, were a feature of the 1940s, revealing the long gloves that women wore with both day and evening clothes.

Dress   **£200–250/$300–400**

Lingerie

The silhouette for the 1940s was short and boxy, a shape determined by wartime restrictions rather than design innovations. Lace trimmings and other decorations disappeared, and fastenings were made from recycled scrap metal – rust can prove a problem for the collector! Nylon stockings were available from around 1940, but in Europe supplies were very restricted throughout the decade. To overcome this some women stained their legs, drew "seams" to imitate stockings, and wore ankle socks. This absence of stockings meant that roll-ons for shaping and flattening the figure had nothing to anchor them in place – they often ended up as roll-ups. French-style knickers were worn with bras under slips, and peach, the fashionable colour of previous decades, was still in vogue. The hourglass shape of Edwardian times returned in the late 1940s, but new techniques and materials meant that the support and control previously achieved with bone and padding was now possible with foam rubber and lightweight synthetics. Even so, comfort still took second place to style.

◆ A beautiful example of strapless hourglass shaping. Strapless bras became common in the 1950s, although the style dates as far back as the 1930s. This satin and lace bra fastens down the back with hooks and eyes. This shape looks back to the Edwardian era, but the stretch inserts at the sides and lightweight plastic boning would only have been possible from the 1940s.

£30–50/$50–80　*Strapless bra*

◆ "Art silk" was introduced in 1910 by the American Viscose Company; in war, silk was needed for parachutes, so artificial silk knickers like these were common. The blue edging and coloured embroidery put this pair of knickers outside the Utility scheme, so it would have been rather expensive. Embroidering was a popular pastime in the 1940s, so lingerie was often hand decorated, but this pair was commercially produced and machine stitched.

French knickers　**£30–50/$50–80**

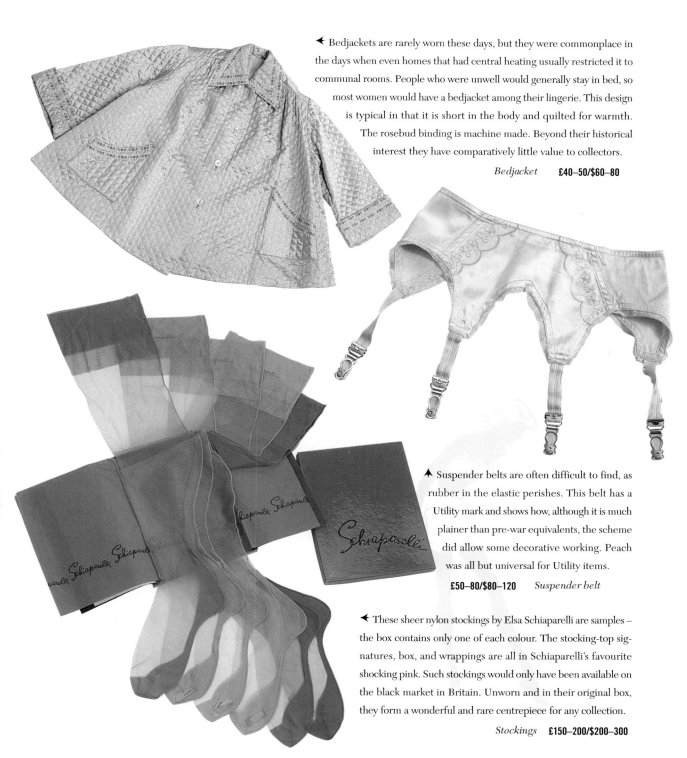

◄ Bedjackets are rarely worn these days, but they were commonplace in the days when even homes that had central heating usually restricted it to communal rooms. People who were unwell would generally stay in bed, so most women would have a bedjacket among their lingerie. This design is typical in that it is short in the body and quilted for warmth. The rosebud binding is machine made. Beyond their historical interest they have comparatively little value to collectors.

Bedjacket   **£40–50/$60–80**

▲ Suspender belts are often difficult to find, as rubber in the elastic perishes. This belt has a Utility mark and shows how, although it is much plainer than pre-war equivalents, the scheme did allow some decorative working. Peach was all but universal for Utility items.

£50–80/$80–120   *Suspender belt*

◄ These sheer nylon stockings by Elsa Schiaparelli are samples – the box contains only one of each colour. The stocking-top signatures, box, and wrappings are all in Schiaparelli's favourite shocking pink. Such stockings would only have been available on the black market in Britain. Unworn and in their original box, they form a wonderful and rare centrepiece for any collection.

Stockings   **£150–200/$200–300**

Accessories

In the 1940s, "making do" meant wearing the same accessories with a range of outfits. As a result, darker hues were, at least temporarily, more practical and adaptable than the carefully matched colours of the inter-war years. Synthetic fabrics replaced leather and the more exotic animal skins such as snake or crocodile in shoes and handbags. The use of black patent leather for shoes and bags was another development from this time. The great shoe designer Ferragamo (1898–1960) made a virtue out of necessity with his "Invisible Shoe" of 1947 – this had a kid heel, but the uppers were made of nylon threads which were completely see-through. The Nazi invasion of France shifted the centre of design from Paris to New York, and, as clean American lines started to replace the softer, more elaborate clothes of the 1930s, accessories followed suit. The influence of military styles was soon felt on civvy street – berets or peaked caps gave any outfit a jaunty military chic. Aage Thaarup (1906–87) was the milliner of the decade – his "Teen" and "Twenty" ranges of hats were mass-produced and sold all over the world.

◄ Handbags such as this one in fake snakeskin were roomy – they had to hold the paraphernalia of wartime, such as the family's ration books. The handle is of a length suitable for wearing over the arm, leaving the hands free for that other essential, the shopping basket. Typically, it has only one small extra section inside, made by stitching an extra piece of rayon to the main lining – none of the purses, pockets, or mirrors of earlier times.

Handbag   **£100–120/$150–200**

▼ Flat shoes were both practical and stylish, and the casual slip-on, introduced in the 1940s, remained popular long after the war. This pair was made under the Utility scheme, and carries the trademark on the inside of the upper. It clearly takes its inspiration from the contemporary wedge styles. The most fashionable and most famous style of wedge was made by "Joyce", the California-based company.

Tan loafers   **£100–150/$150–200**

➤ Hats, like fur, were not rationed – such was their scarcity
they did not need to be. Women often knitted their own hats,
and the turban was still popular, now as a way of keeping hair
under control. The dyed feathers on the blue felt hat on the
left come from larger domestic birds. rather than the
imported rarities of earlier decades; the green velvet
version has plenty of room inside for piled-up hair.
Military chic made berets – previously worn only by the
armed forces – popular with everyone, usually puffed up for an
"inflated" look. Most stylish of all is the black felt hat on the
right, with its peak, pleats, and ribbon trimmings.

£80–120/$120–180   *Blue hat with feather*

Green velvet beret   **£120–180/$180–220**

£100–150/$150–200   *Black felt hat*

➤ The unworn blue Utility shoes (left) are made of recycled
material treated to look like snakeskin. Under the scheme, heels
were restricted to a maximum height of five cm (two inches) and,
like all Utility items, these carry the scheme's stamp. In this
example the stamp is embossed on the sole, although it is more
usually found on the inside of the shoe. The pair on the right
dates from about 1940 and, with high heels, pale green leather,
and glass bead decoration, would have been very expensive.

£120–180/$180–220   *Blue shoes (unworn)*

Green shoes   **£150–180/$180–220**

Menswear

Until the late 1940s men's fashions were subject to even more limitations than those of women. The demand for military uniforms was such that wool for civilian clothing was in short supply everywhere – even in the USA. The Vichy government in France declared that men's coats and jackets were to have no pleats, darted pockets, or yokes. Double-breasted suits and shawl collars were also prohibited, and trousers had to have a maximum width at the ankle of ten and a half inches. Early signs of teenage rebellion are identifiable in the popularity of the brightly coloured zoot suits, originally worn by young black men in America. These had trousers which were exceptionally wide at the knee but tapered to a narrow ankle, and had wide-shouldered, narrow-waisted, long, draped jackets. "Za zou, za zou, zay", a catch-phrase of the flamboyant jazz musician Cab Calloway, is thought to be the origin of the name "Zazous", given in France to young male followers of the style.

◄ All these ties are unworn, and are in the long style favoured during the 1940s – the middle one, by Tootal, still has its original price label. Trousers were usually held up by braces rather than belts, and, as essential items of clothing, braces were available with prices and quality both strictly controlled under the Utility scheme. Even so, their high content of sought-after elastic made them difficult to find.

£30–50/$50–70   *Braces (per pair)*

£40–60/$60–80   *Ties (each)*

◄ These unworn, tan leather boots are typical of men's footwear in the 1940s, although they tend towards the functional rather than fashionable. In the late 1940s the American armed forces sold off millions of items of army surplus in Europe – the first time that khaki and other army staples became fashionable. British uniform, especially the duffel coat, also gained fashion status, especially when taken up later by the American "beat" poet Allen Ginsberg and by many young French intellectuals.

Boots (unworn)   **£50–70/$70–100**

↞ Soft cotton and wide, pointed, integral collars mark these shirts as typical of the time. Coloured shirts had become commonplace during the 1920s, so stripes caused no comment at all by the 1940s. In fact a craze for brightly contrasting checks had briefly taken hold in France at the end of the war, only to be superseded by a craze for dirty corduroy versions and anything else that the French existentialists decreed was "anti-fashion".

£50–70/$70–100   *Shirts (unworn)*

➤ Double-breasted suits such as this were permissible under the Utility scheme, as were contrasting colours in check. Turn-ups could not be included on trousers made to measure, but a pair otherwise too long had to be worn with turn-ups rather than trimmed to the correct length.

£150–200/$220–280   *Suit*

↞ This style and design is known as Fair Isle, and such hand-knitted pullovers for men had been very popular since the 1920s. Knitted in fine two-ply wool, this one, however, is definitely from the 1940s. New techniques in processing raw materials meant that in the post-war era wool did not shrink when washed. However, with older yarns this is always a risk, and even cold water washing will not prevent it, so dry cleaning or, if fragile, hanging on a clothes-line to air, are preferable.

£50–80/$80–120   *Pullover*

The Fifties

Living standards improved rapidly during the 1950s, and launderettes and home washing machines made looking after clothes easier. The American influence was everywhere but its impact, through rock 'n' roll, was especially strong on the young. Italian styling was the new force in fashion, but established designers held their own. Dior remained the most influential, but Cristobal Balenciaga, a Spaniard who came to Paris during the Spanish Civil War, developed the Dior look using a simple cut and line to suit taller women. Hubert Givenchy worked with Balenciaga, coming to prominence designing clothes for Audrey Hepburn in the 1954 film Sabrina Fair. Hepburn's short, sculpted tops had "bateau" necklines and cropped sleeves – with her slight figure and dark, fringed hair she epitomized the fashionable ideal of the pretty urchin, the "gamine". At the other extreme was Marilyn Monroe: furs, diamonds, high heels, and plunging necklines were her trademarks, effectively summing up the aspirations and the affluence of the day.

Daywear

Pierre Balmain was a leader in 1950s haute couture, alongside Dior and Balenciaga. While Dior was concentrating on ultra-feminine styling, his two rivals were experimenting with tailored clothes and waistlines. Balmain became famous in the late 1950s for his "Sac" dress, which echoed the draped and low-waisted styles of World War I and the 1920s. By the mid-1950s all three designers had taken up the "A-line", in which garments flared from the bust or waist making a triangle-like shape, with the hem of the garment as the third side. A casual, sophisticated approach, inspired by Italian styling and encouraged by increased leisure time, made separates as popular as dresses. Women of all ages wore tapering trousers which could be full or mid-calf length, or fall just below the knee – the latter were known as "pirate pants". An American heiress from Philadelphia, Grace Kelly, was one of the most photographed exponents of this cool, sophisticated style; she went from model to film star and, finally, to royal fashion icon when she married Prince Rainier of Monaco.

➤ Close-fitting, tapered trousers with short tops were popular with all age groups, but the style was most suited to the teenage market. "Pedal pushers" – loose, calf-length trousers, often with turn-ups – were an especially popular development. Tops could be matching, as in this example, but equally commonplace were sophisticated Italian prints in bright colours and patterns.

£80–120/$120–180
Trousers and top

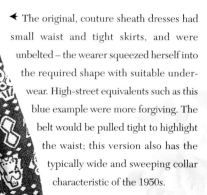

◄ The original, couture sheath dresses had small waist and tight skirts, and were unbelted – the wearer squeezed herself into the required shape with suitable underwear. High-street equivalents such as this blue example were more forgiving. The belt would be pulled tight to highlight the waist; this version also has the typically wide and sweeping collar characteristic of the 1950s.

£100–150/$150–200
Sheath-style dress

◄ Balmain (1914–82) designed a range of dresses for younger women with full underskirts of stiffened net, topped with lace or tulle, which clearly inspired this high-street version. Balmain was very influential in America during the 1950s, when he opened a chain of ps selling ready-to-wear designs. This dress is in blue voile, with white ocking decoration and paste buttons – such buttons featured on many 1950s garments, a nod in the direction of more affluent lifestyles.

Blue dress   **£100–150/$150–200**

► Cotton examples of the full-skirted 1950s dress were popular because they were bright and cheery for summer, and are sought after today for the same reason. Designs were printed on every fabric imaginable, and all-over patterns, such as the blue-print dress opposite, and the floral print seen here, are typical of the 1950s.

£70–100/$100–150

Cotton floral print dress

◄ This nylon print dress has taffeta underslips and would have been very crisp when new. To maintain its stiffness it needed to be lightly starched and ironed into shape. This dress still has its original belt, which always enhances the value. In the mid-1950s, floral designs were championed by London couturiers such as Victor Stiebel (1907–96), who designed clothes for members of the British royal family to wear at race meetings at Ascot.

Rose print dress   **£120–180/$180–220**

Fine wool and a fur collar, fastened with a glitzy clasp – this cardigan says everything about 1950s glamour. Made in the USA by Abrahams, it proclaims unashamed luxury. Fur – imitation or real – was a recurrent feature of 1950s styling and was often added to collars and cuffs.

Cardigan   **£100–150/$150–200**

If you could not afford fur, you could make do with a variety of alternatives – in this case, a synthetic leopard-skin print. Mink was the most expensive and most sought-after fur, but leopard and ocelot were also popular alternatives. Fur-trimmed garments are typical of 1950s high fashion, but modern attitudes towards fur makes them less popular with collectors, so prices are often lower than might be expected. This wool suit has no fastenings – a nod in the direction of the swing coats and swagger jackets which remained fashionable from the late 1940s onwards.

Suit   **£80–120/$120–180**

This wool jacket has a satin trim and padded shoulders, and is labelled "100 per cent worsted Barathea". It was worn by the actress Joanna Lumley in the television drama *Nancherrow*. Many 1950s jackets fitted very closely to the body and were accompanied by a simple scarf or a string of pearls – depending on how low the neckline plunged!

£100–150/$150–220   *Jacket*

➤ Embroidered cardigans were part of a demand for fancy knitwear which suited fun 1950s fashion. New mass-production techniques made possible reasonably priced, machine-knitted items in elaborate designs. Polo-neck and angora sweaters were particularly popular with teenagers. Mixtures of synthetic and natural fibres meant that woollen garments kept their shapes better and were more hardwearing. Acrylic fibres were launched in 1947 under the trademarks of Orlon and Acrilan, but it was only in the 1950s that demand grew.

£80–120/$120–180   *Cardigan*

◄ From a collector's point of view, an unworn garment, with all the original labels, is worth more than something second-hand and used. This skirt, from an American sportswear range, is made of a cotton mixture, with a kick pleat at the front and a generous cut to encourage easy movement. Clare McCardell (1905–58), the first internationally acclaimed American designer, led the way in the 1940s and 50s with designs for everyday use based on sportswear.

£50–80/$80–120   *Skirt*

➤ A wonderfully full skirt, just the thing to swirl around while dancing "at the hop". Cats, leopards, and poodles were the most popular animals with 1950s designers, and often appeared in humorous settings. This skirt, clearly aimed at the teenage market, has several classic features: the use of appliqué, of mottoes, and of decorative braiding which here forms the lead and collar on "the little cat". Some of the cat's features have now disappeared, along with the skirt's original belt, which obviously diminishes the garment's value, but the style is irresistible.

Cat skirt   **£100–150/$150–200**

Eveningwear

With increased leisure time and more money to spend, many women in the 1950s experimented with different evening styles. For formal occasions women still wore floor-length ball gowns, but in cuts varying from the wide-skirted, tight-waisted New Look to the body-hugging sheath dress. Shiny satins were sprinkled with sequins and rhinestones, and attention focused on the bust. With strapless gowns in particular, support for the figure was essential, and many came with integral boning and stiff net petticoats. The American designer Charles James was at the height of his popularity. Working in New York, he regarded his dresses as works of art and produced fabulously sculpted ball gowns in opulent fabrics which today can fetch huge sums at auction. Shorter-length cocktail dresses also came into vogue, and Chanel rejected the "boned horrors" of fashionable couture to produce relaxed evening styles. When teamed with glamorous tops, elegantly tapered trousers were also fashionable eveningwear, but it was considered distinctly vulgar to combine them with high heels.

◄ Cardigans such as this heavily embroidered and beaded version were popular for eveningwear, especially when teamed with gold slippers or mules. Tight jumpers and cardigans were worn by all ages, but even knitwear had its rebellious side. The loose-fitting "Sloppy Joe" was adopted by younger people, especially art students, often seen as subversive at the time. The influence of radical politics on fashion was a phenomenon that began to dominate youth style from the 1950s. But whereas links between political thought and fashion are explicitly acknowledged by French intellectuals, their British counterparts have tended to reject such concerns as frivolous.

Cardigan £80–120/$120–180

Evening slippers £40–60/$60–80

◄ This sheath dress, with its flying panel and "bateau" neckline, would have been the choice of the younger, more fashionable woman. The tight fit and short length meant, however, that the style was of no use to the keen dancer until the early 1960s, when the Twist became the latest hit on the dance floors. Flying panels were popular, featuring on both short and full-length eveningwear in the same or contrasting materials.

Dress £100–150/$150–200

➤ The revival of crinolines provided a more traditional style for the evening, and was encouraged by the new freedom that synthetic materials allowed. This dress, in nylon net over taffeta skirts with white taffeta petticoats, is typical. Its four stiff hoops in "Flexicrine (British Patent)" give the skirt its shape and, like many evening dresses of the time, it can stand on its own, supported only by its stiffened taffeta and its rigid frame. The garment is labelled as "Maryon" by "Ricci Michaels Ltd" of Mayfair, London.

Crinoline dress   **£150–200/$220–280**

◄ This ball gown in black cotton net is encrusted with sequins, another typically exuberant 1950s trimming for eveningwear and accessories. Made to measure for the original owner, it has a shaped and padded bust, and the underskirt has three layers of stiff net, one layer of starched black muslin, and a taffeta underslip.

£100–150/$150–200   *Black gown (damaged)*

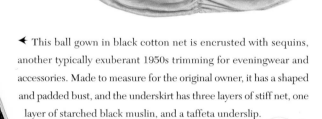

➤ The nylon net over satin taffeta makes this dress, with its flying panel, an archetypal "prom" dress for a teenage girl. These dresses were so named because girls wore them for the formal dances known as "proms" (from promenades) attended by high school students in America. Stiffly starched and pressed, "prom" dresses were worn with swept-up hair and little white gloves.

£80–120/$120–180   *"Prom" dress*

Lingerie

Lingerie in the 1950s had its work cut out with the considerable demands made on the average female figure by the variety of fashionable silhouettes. Bulges had nowhere to hide in the sheath dress, so seamless, all-in-one foundation garments were essential to achieve the required slim waist and hips and the exaggerated shoulders. Marilyn Monroe made curves fashionable, however, and large breasts were another facet of the decade's preferred shape. The eccentric film producer Howard Hughes used his experience as an engineer to design a cantilevered bra for the film star Jane Russell to wear in *The Outlaw*. The film was banned for its scenes featuring her cleavage, although Russell later claimed not to have worn the Hughes bra as it was too uncomfortable. Bras were generally pointed, with rows of circle stitching to preserve their shape. Padded or even inflatable bras enhanced the bust, but women were warned against wearing the latter in pressurized planes. Girdles, "waspies", and suspender belts were employed to flatten the midriff and hips, and yards of petticoat were essential for special occasions.

▲ This bra is by Gossard, an American company founded at the beginning of the 20th century, which originally made corsets. Despite the beguiling name given on the label, "Silk Skin", it is made from a fairly stiff mixture of cotton and nylon, reinforced by the rows and rows of stitching on the cups.

Bra   **£50–80/$80–120**

◄ Nylons had, strictly speaking, been around since 1938. The name is supposed to have derived from combining New York and London, where scientists working on the product were based. The DuPont company started manufacturing nylon stockings in 1939, but the outbreak of war prevented their sale outside the USA. American soldiers were the main source of supply in Europe until after the war, and even then scarce clothing coupons were needed for the few pairs available. The demand was especially great for sheer stockings such as these. The embroidered heels add to the value. It is unlikely they have ever been worn; nylons like this were – and still are – very fragile.

Stockings   **£40–60/$60–80**

These two nightdresses are of very contrasting styles but are both very collectable. Floral-print versions are particularly popular with teenage enthusiasts for vintage fashion, who wear them as an expression of the trend for floral, feminine designs. The red night-dress is in layers of nylon and of a type more readily associated with the 1950s. Négligées in matching materials are a feature of the period, and a set would obviously be more valuable.

£50–80/$80–120   *Floral nightdress*

Red nightdress   **£40–60/$60–80**

Imagine this beautiful trio of petticoats added to those volu-minous 1950s ball gowns, and the source of the impossible fullness of such dresses becomes clear. These three petticoats in varieties of stiff net would rustle through doorways and fill the back seat of any luxury car. Lace and net petticoats are very prone to damage, and the collector should check for any torn areas before buying.

Petticoats (each)   **£40–80 /$60–120**

Accessories

Italian styling had its greatest impact on accessories: smooth, soft leather handbags and elaborately styled shoes were a direct result of the Italian influence spread by such film stars as Sophia Loren and Gina Lollobrigida. Bags came in all sorts of materials, and the fascination with new plastics especially meant that the finished items did not imitate traditional, natural materials as they had in the 1940s. Small, close-fitting hats were particularly popular, but berets, now worn in a flat, pancake shape, were common before 1955, along with hats of all shapes and sizes. Hairstyles specifically suited to the teenage market came to the fore from the middle of the decade onwards; a swinging pony-tail was fine for dancing to rock 'n' roll records, and younger people no longer routinely wore hats as their parents had done. Older women preferred their hair in a French pleat or in the puffed-up style known as the "chrysanthemum cut", which in turn created a trend for cossack or drum-shaped hats. Stoles made from fur or from brightly coloured fabrics were worn at all times of the day.

➤ ➤ A smooth and stylish handbag in red plastic: the original owner would have matched it to her shoes, hat, and gloves. The glasses have classic wing frames, which had the effect of making the wearer appear ten years older. The red frames are pearlized, with brass fittings, while the black ones are decorated with false marcasite, a crystal which, along with diamanté and rhinestones, remained popular thoroughout the decade.

Glasses   **£15–50/$25–80**   *Handbag*   **£120–180/$180–220**

➤ Raffia, wickerwork, and fake fruit brought exuberance and frivolity to handbags in the mid-1950s. On this example the amazing quantity of fruit becomes the design rather than just being a feature of it. Fake flowers and fruit did not appear as much on handbags again until Lulu Guinness's creations of the late 1990s. These 1950s versions are prone to damage, as the wire and light cloth or paper of the fruit and its fixtures have become fragile over time. You can expect to pay a high price for an example in good condition.

Fruit handbag   **£150–220/$220–280**

➤ Strapless shoes or slippers known as mules were introduced during the 1940s, however it was not until the 1950s that they became popular. Freed from wartime restrictions, shoe designers experimented with bright, multi-coloured designs and fabrics. This beautiful pair, with matching handbag, is typical of the styles demanded by younger people. Of five million teenagers in Britain in 1956, four million worked, earning incomes 50 per cent higher on average than those of their pre-war counterparts. *Vogue* caught this trend, and its British edition soon had pages dedicated to fashions for younger readers.

£180–220/$220–280   *Coloured mules and matching handbag*

➤ Feet had a bad time in the 1950s: court shoes with high heels and rounded toes were superseded by even higher stiletto heels and pointed "winkle-picker" toes. The heels forced the weight onto the front of the foot, squashing toes together and causing bunions. Stilettos played havoc with soft linoleum floors and were banned from public buildings. They caught in gratings in the street, too, and were so susceptible to damage that heel bars offering instant repairs sprang up in towns. While you were wearing them, however, stilettos looked absolutely fabulous, as this glamorous pair, in embossed and punched coloured leathers, shows.

Shoes   **£120–180/$180–220**

➤➤ A dramatic statement in accessories, these Perspex mules would make painted toenails and a pedicure essential. These shoes echo the famous "Invisible Shoe" of 1947. By 1957 its designer, Salvatore Ferragamo, had already registered 350 patents for shoe designs, and had created 20,000 styles. Handbags with shoulder straps came into fashion at this time, and the twisted rope handle is as innovatory as the clear, frameless bag.

£300–400/$450–550   *Perspex mules and matching handbag*

Menswear

Menswear in the 1950s was often sober and traditional in its styling, but there were signs of a more relaxed and colourful approach: bowling shirts, and the craze for bowling alleys, took off first in America and then in Britain. Jeans, firmly classed as workwear for their first hundred years, now had fashion status. British officers went to Savile Row in London, where tailors still measured them for narrow trousers and longer, draped jackets with velvet collars and single-button fastenings, worn under smart Crombie overcoats. This style was adapted from Edwardian menswear, and was popularized in the mid-1950s by working-class London boys known as "Teddy Boys". An influential, and essentially urban, fashion, this evolved into the "Mod" style of the 1960s, just as the scruffier, bike-related 1950s parallel, "Greasers", developed into the 1960s "Rockers". Smart men sported sharp Italian suits which had short, "bum-freezer" jackets with wide shoulders, and close-fitting, tapered trousers, all worn with narrow, straight ties, and shoes with pointed toes, called "winkle-pickers".

◄ Labour shortages in the 1950s meant that jobs were available. Wages rose, and many teenage boys chose to spend their money on a "bomber" or "varsity" jacket. With its high waist, and elasticated cuffs and collar, it was first worn by American pilots. College boys wore brightly coloured, satin versions, and so an alternative name, the "varsity" jacket, evolved. American films played a large part in defining the teenage image, especially James Dean with his white T-shirt, red Harrington jacket, and Levis in *Rebel Without a Cause* and Marlon Brando with his T-shirt, zipped leather jacket, and peaked cap in *The Wild One*.

£120–180/$180–220   *"Varsity" jacket*

▼ The working-class "Teddy Boys" were named after their passion for Edwardian styling, which they combined with touches of American glamour. Long drape jackets, trimmed with velvet, were worn with boot-lace ties, short drainpipe trousers, and "brothel creepers" – crêpe-soled shoes popular during the war. They also wore sideburns and "D.A." ("duck's arse") haircuts, imitating those of rock 'n' rollers Carl Perkins and Elvis Presley. This jacket is clearly from the 1950s because, unlike later revival versions, its velvet cuffs turn back.

£120–180/$180–220
Drape jacket

◄ The American influence in fashion resulted in the popularity of wide, loud-patterned ties, often in the new synthetic fabrics. The tie on the right conceals a pin-up – the term derives from World War II, when servicemen pinned up pictures of favourite actresses. The popularity of pin-ups spread in the 1950s, first in magazines such as *Esquire*, which famously featured those by the artist Varga, and then in menswear – clothes with pin-up motifs are very collectable today.

Ties (each) **£20–30/$30–50**

↗ Brocade waistcoats have always implied affluence, but this taffeta-lined example is especially rich. In the 1950s, new styles in suits and jackets created a strong demand for such fancy waistcoats. The upper-class originators of the Edwardian revival would wear plain, double-breasted waistcoats with wide lapels as part of three-piece suits, but others favoured less formal styles.

Waistcoat **£50–80/$80–120**

↙ The popularity of American, square-cut bowling styles and of bright Hawaiian prints meant that shirts were no longer automatically worn with ties. Given such licence, the fashionable man looked for leisure shirts with short sleeves, pockets, contrasting colours, and trimmings. Both the shirts shown here are in mixtures of cotton, wool, and synthetic fabrics. The brown shirt is more valuable because it was made in the USA, in this case by a company called "Two Legs Inc".

Brown shirt **£80–120/$120–180**   *Green shirt* **£60–80/$90–120**

THE SIXTIES

In the 1960s, simply to be young was to be fashionable. In another interesting parallel with the 1920s, shorter skirts and a boyish look again became de rigueur *for young women. The decade began fairly quietly, although one American innovation, the beehive hairstyle, finally ended the hat's role as essential daywear. The fashion leader was Jackie Kennedy, wife of President John F. Kennedy, who typified youthful chic. She designed her own Chanel-inspired suits, made for her by Oleg Cassini, and paired them with small "pillbox" hats by Halston. "Swinging London" was the centre of teenage fashion, especially around Carnaby Street and King's Road. Mary Quant, with her short skirts, skinny rib jumpers, and coloured tights, was the most prominent of the young British designers bypassing established couture houses and designing low-priced garments for all. In Paris, Yves Saint Laurent caused outrage with his "Left Bank Beat Look" inspired by street style, but pop stars were now more influential on fashion than designers or film stars, and the hippy movement liberated men's clothes to a greater degree than ever before.*

DAYWEAR

The radical changes of the 1960s were reflected in fashion. Sexual mores were altered by the introduction of the contraceptive pill, and the drug culture arrived. The mini-skirt became a symbol of this new climate of liberation. Girls no longer wanted to dress like their mothers, since their youth made them fashionable, and "Swinging London" was now at the heart of teenage revolution. Designer Mary Quant (b.1934), fashion models Jean Shrimpton and Twiggy, and pop stars, most famously the Beatles, spread the message across the world. Photographers such as David Bailey and Lord Snowdon became more influential, shooting models moving around, stressing youth and freedom, with hand-held cameras. To achieve the boyish look, dresses had high waists and side darts, helping to flatten the bust. Street style had taken over to such an extent that Balenciaga (1895–1972) retired in 1968 announcing that couture was dead. Other Paris designers such as Yves Saint Laurent (1936–2008), Paco Rabanne (b.1934), and André Courrèges (b.1923) seized on new shapes and materials, launching collections reflecting the Space Age.

◄ A typical, fresh-looking, 1960s cotton print dress. All-over patterns such as this were made possible by new manufacturing processes introduced during the previous decade, but this design and the bright colours are quintessentially 1960s. Straight shift dresses such as this have a clear connection to Givenchy's "Sac" dress of the late 1950s, but the image conjured up is of a "gamine" rather than elegance and mature sophistication.

Floral dress   **£70–100/$100–150**

◄ Psychedelic patterns, directly inspired by the drug culture, found their way onto the most respectable garments. The use of drugs was not unique to the 1960s, but the perceived teenage element caused a moral panic not seen since the 1920s. This rich silk print dress is very typical of the psychedelic style popular among collectors, and the colours have not faded with age.

£100–150/$150–180

Psychedelic silk dress

◄ This raincoat has a cotton feel but is actually synthetic – fashion raincoats like this were often labelled "showerproof" because they gave little real protection against an English downpour. Genuinely waterproof raincoats were usually made from PVC (polyvinyl chloride), which could be dyed in bright colours. This coat has raglan sleeves, a high waist, and brass buttons. The label is Valstar, a variation on the more famous Valspar, which has been making classic raincoats for generations.

Raincoat   **£70–110/$100–150**

◥ Twiggy was the most famous British model in the 1960s. Her manager, Justin de Villeneuve, launched her in 1966, and before long everyone wanted to look like this knock-kneed, wide-eyed, gawky teenager from Neasden in London. This dress is typical of the style she made popular: in lime-green linen decorated with machine lace, it falls 20 to 25 cm (8 to 10 in) above the knee.

Green shift dress   **£70–110/$100–150**

◄ Curled, "page-boy" hair, big eyes, and flat heels dominated, but even so not all women wanted to look like little girls. Geometric and Space Age styles were also popular, and were encouraged by the contemporary Op Art scene and the Art Deco revival, both of which stressed shape and abstract forms. This coat, with its simple, asymmetrical styling, complements perfectly the medium-heeled, slingback, PVC shoes from Harrods in London.

£120–180/$180–220   *Coat*   **£50–80/$80–120**   *Shoes*

89

➤ Simple, geometric designs featured regularly on 1960s clothes, and this cotton print blouse also has the "little girl" collar that gained popularity at the time. A smart, shirt-style top such as this might be teamed with a pair of still-fashionable narrow trousers in a matching colour for eveningwear. Vidal Sassoon added to this liberated, stylish image with his layered bob cuts which, increasingly during the 1960s, freed women from the tyranny of bouffants and beehives, and their supporting cast of rollers, lacquer and hairpins.

Cotton print blouse   **£30–50/$50–80**

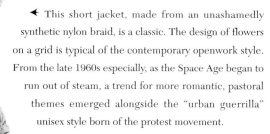

◄ This short jacket, made from an unashamedly synthetic nylon braid, is a classic. The design of flowers on a grid is typical of the contemporary openwork style. From the late 1960s especially, as the Space Age began to run out of steam, a trend for more romantic, pastoral themes emerged alongside the "urban guerrilla" unisex style born of the protest movement.

Jacket   **£40–60/$60–80**

➤ This lurid, fussy blouse is in Terylene (called Dacron in the USA). Terylene was the brand name in Britain for a man-made fibre developed in 1941 by the Calico Printers' Association and produced commercially by Imperial Chemical Industries, better known as ICI. The demand for easy-care fabrics after the war made Terylene very popular, particularly as it was available in almost any colour imaginable – as this vivid example demonstrates!

Terylene blouse   **£20–30/$30–50**

◄ This PVC raincoat has the Courrèges logo in white prominently on its front, and it is also woven into the removable artificial silk façonné lining. André Courrèges worked with Balenciaga, and in the 1960s became famous worldwide as the "Space Age designer". He used clean, futuristic lines and man-made materials to produce his see-through dresses, shiny catsuits, silver spangled trousers, goggles, and famous short white boots.

Courrèges raincoat
£750–1250/$1200–1800

↗ The mini had lost its trendy shock impact by the end of the 1960s, and this skirt is an example of one new length which was beginning to take its place. Made of bouclé fibre in a mohair, wool, and synthetic mix, the style of its leather decoration, together with the synthetic mixture fabric, identify it as a product of the 1960s. Made in Austria, it is labelled as "Exi wholesale couture".

Bouclé skirt   **£60–80/$90–130**

➤ André Courrèges, Mary Quant, and John Bates (b.1938) are all credited with inventing and popularizing the mini-skirt, and leather versions such as this have retained their appeal with collectors over the decades. Less well-known than Courrèges or Quant, Bates designed outfits for Diana Rigg who, as Emma Peel in the cult television series *The Avengers*, was the archetypal 1960s liberated woman. Bates also popularized the use of Op Art print fabrics. The use of Op Art in fashion was inspired in particular by the pioneering work of the abstract painter Bridget Riley, who used basic, repeated shapes in her work to give an impression of movement.

Mini-skirt   **£70–100/$100–150**

Eveningwear

Bright colours and Op Art featured alongside more traditional, full-length and ball-gown styles for eveningwear. Large, long ear-rings, theatrically false eyelashes, and heavy make-up were even more prevalent than during the day. Going out at night now also meant dancing at the newly popular discothèques, and styles reflected this craze. Among younger people especially, there was often no clear distinction between day and evening clothes – only the accessories changed. In the early 1960s common styles for eveningwear ranged from pinafores to sheath dresses – in 1960 *Vogue* reported that the "quirk" for the year was to wear a long coat over a short dress. Although the radical changes which would affect 1960s fashion were clearly under way early in the decade, they did not filter down to the High Street for a few years. So large busts and small waists continued to be the desired shape, and back-combed and lacquered hair might well be held in place with a velvet hairband, a very popular accessory throughout this time.

➤ A full-length shift with the typical 1960s flattened bust. Like most eveningwear of this time, the dress is labelled "Dry Clean Only". Dry cleaning was such big business in the 1960s that the long-established firm of Sketchley advertised on television. Dry cleaning vintage garments is not, despite the label, always a good idea – the rigours of heavy pressing and chemicals can knock the life out of a fabric.

£70–110/$100–150

Pink dress

◄ A clear continuation of 1950s dress styles, in which layers of taffeta or similar material would be supported by stiffened petticoats. This example, with its enormous bows on the skirt, is from the house of Dior, which adds to its value. Christian Dior died in 1957, but his influence here is discernible: black was a particularly favoured colour. Of the designers who have followed at Dior, John Galliano has perhaps been closest to him in spirit.

Dress **£800–1200/$1200–1800**

➤ This short lurex dress is by C & A, one of a number of British High Street chain stores which began to cater for younger people, and which, with their music and lighting, were more like discos than conventional women's clothing retailers. This dress, in lurex, is obviously for a more formal occasion. The new short length was very popular with younger women but, like the trouser suit, would not have been accepted at every establishment.

£50–80/$80–120

Short dress

➤ A new informality led to novel approaches such as knitted eveningwear, here in a lurex fleck wool. It also demonstrates another innovation – although in one piece, it gives the impression of being a long skirt and separate top. Always check for signs of damage or wear around the armpits in close-fitting, knitted styles. Damage here is almost impossible to repair.

Knitted dress   **£70–110/$100–150**

➤ This pretty pink concoction has a full skirt, and incorporates a shoulder sash in the same material; it is labelled "Radcliffe Chapman, Grovesnor St". High-heeled court shoes and a matching handbag were essential accessories for the early 1960s look, as was the back-combed "beehive" hairstyle created in America.

£100–150/$150–200   *Pink dress*

Lingerie

Underwear entered the throwaway age in the 1960s, with the introduction of cheap new fabrics. In just ten years the idea of repairing underwear and darning socks became a preoccupation of the previous generation. The range and purpose of underwear also changed dramatically during this time: foundation garments, with their double fastenings of hooks and eyes under a zip, were near universal in the 1950s, but by the end of the 1960s these traditional styles were worn almost entirely by women old enough to have grown up with them. Most women, however, had roll-ons or the widely advertised Playtex girdles. The new silhouette, most fashionably displayed by models such as Twiggy and Jean Shrimpton, was of a thin, near-childlike figure with a flattened chest – it certainly did not come naturally to most women. Probably the most influential and outrageous designer of lingerie at this time was Rudi Gernreich (1922–85), who invented the topless bathing suit, the "no-bra" bra, in several variations, and also the flesh-coloured body stocking.

➤ This is the type of foundation garment so reviled by the women's liberation movement in the 1960s. A magnificent example of double fastenings and firm, but not painful, control, it kept the wearer warm as well as in shape. The bra moulds the bust in a manner more typical of the 1950s. As the decade progressed, most women replaced all-in-one foundation garments such as this with a girdle or roll-on, which flattened both hips and midriff. The Playtex Living Girdle, using both Lycra and Spandex, was a best-seller throughout the 1960s.

£80–120/$120–180 *Foundation garment*

➤ A wonderful example of the "baby doll" style of nightdress in black nylon, with a white nylon lining. This model is by Wolsey, an established British firm which, among other innovations, introduced thick, woolly tights in 1960. "Baby doll" nighties are closely associated with the Swinging Sixties, but they take their name from the 1956 shocker *Baby Doll*, in which the actress Carroll Baker wore the garment. This type of nightdress is worth more if it has the original matching knickers.

Nightdress   **£50–80/$80–120**

► A definite contrast to the whirlpool-stitched, lift-and-separate styles of earlier decades, this is a classic 1960s bra by Maidenform. Founded in the USA during the 1920s by two dressmakers, Maidenform flourished in the 1950s and 60s. This padded nylon bra is in excellent condition; it carries the label of approval from the International Ladies Garment Workers Union, and was made in America under union conditions.

Bra   **£20–30/$30–50**

◄ A beautiful little cotton-mixture slip – whatever else they discarded, women and girls all wore underslips. Today's enthusiasts often wear these as dresses. The flatter and more youthful look, and the focus on the youth market by designers like Mary Quant, both helped to encourage and develop teenage markets for lingerie, and for bras in particular. The bra slip was an innovation which first gained a foothold in the early 1960s.

Slip   **£30–40/$45–60**

► This pink concoction is in nylon, with plastic shapings and an underwired bra. Underwiring in bras dates back to the 19th century, and even modern equivalents are not without their hazards – the cook Clarissa Dickson-Wright recalled how she once thought she was having a heart attack, only to find that her chest pain was caused by the wire in her bra working loose during some particularly enthusiastic dancing!

Bustier   **£45–45/$70–90**

◄ These stockings are one of those essential items for anyone collecting 1960s fashions: Mary Quant began to produce her own stockings and tights in the 1960s, with her distinctive daisy logo on the packs. Her patterned and lacy designs were almost inevitable accompaniments to her mini-skirts and dresses.

Stockings   **£15–25/$25–40**

ACCESSORIES

Designers who had commandeered plastics, paper, metals, and mirrors for garments had no hesitation in seizing the opportunities offered by the new synthetics for hats, handbags, and shoes. In 1967 Dior models wore Perspex heels, and the leather-look "Corform" – a plastic substitute which the makers, DuPont, claimed would enable feet to breathe – was being widely used in the USA, France, and Britain. Calf-length and knee-length fashion boots were worn with miniskirts. Hats were no longer compulsory or formal – PVC headgear was made to match outfits, and ciré, renamed "Wet Look Leather", had something of a revival. Women used shoulder bags instead of carrying handbags, and, if they felt like wearing gloves, might choose fingerless mittens. The popularity of separates meant that mixing and matching was frivolous and fun. From the late 1960s the influence of the hippy movement lead to an explosion of interest in clothes indigenous to South America, Mexico, Africa, the Far East, and Eastern Europe. Demand for accessories in those styles followed as the ethnic look took over.

⤷ The handbag with the Union Jack design is plastic with a nylon moiré lining. The Union Jack was a frequent motif on clothes and accessories, reflecting a fascination with "Swinging London", and was further popularized by England winning the World Cup in 1966. The "I'm Backing Britain" campaign, urging people to support the economy, also made liberal use of the Union Jack, and related badges, T-shirts, and memorabilia are very collectable. The plastic and raffia combination on the other bag is very artificial in character and therefore also very 1960s.

Union Jack bag   **£40–60/$60–80**

Raffia bag   **£30–40/$40–60**

◂ Matching shoes and handbag sets such as this were used for formal occasions. The bag has a shoulder strap, a feature almost unknown a decade earlier. High heels did not suit either trousers or a boyish look, so shoes were flatter, with mid-height heels, slingbacks, and square-shaped toes. The vibrant colours are pure psychedelia.

Shoes and bag   **£250–350/$400–500**

↗ Eyes were the focus of the face in the 1960s: heavy make-up and huge, false eyelashes were employed to make them appear big. Lips were kept pale to avoid distracting attention from the eyes, and sunglasses also played their part, often offset by big plastic ear-rings. Dayglo colours, as seen in the pink and orange pair, are especially collectable. In the late 1960s, the "Owl" look arrived, with large, round glasses, as in the red plastic pair here, and eye make-up to match.

Red sunglasses in case **£50–80/$80–120**

Dayglo sunglasses **£60–90/$90–130**

↗ Fashion watches had brightly coloured faces in unusual shapes, and often quite heavy leather straps. Fashion designers produced their own ranges, and these command higher prices than mass-market examples. The watch on the extreme left has a Pop Art face typical of the period.

Watches (each) **£25–35/$40–60**

↗ Most women wore hats only for formal occasions in the 1960s, and these did not depart radically from traditional shapes and styles. However, the beret underwent one of its many revivals when Faye Dunaway wore one in the film *Bonnie and Clyde*. This style of exaggerated floppy cap was made popular by the folk singer Donovan and John Lennon of the Beatles. Worn by both men and women, it was casual but could also keep long hair under control.

Hat **£20–30/$30–50**

➤ Courrèges, in keeping with his Space Age theme, showed his mini-dresses in all-white showrooms, where the models wore white, mid-calf boots, with zippers on the inside. Yves Saint Laurent took designs from the paintings of Mondrian (themselves based on the New York city grid) and put them on accessories and also on his spare, straight-cut dresses.

£200–300/$300–500 *Boots*

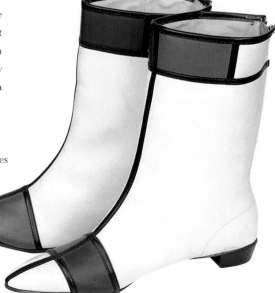

Menswear

Men had their own fashion revolution in the 1960s, freed at last from constraints of the post-war era such as army haircuts and "demob" suits. In 1957 John Stephen opened his first menswear store in Carnaby Street, then a dingy alley but soon to become the most famous shopping street in the world. Jake Arnott, recalling the 1960s in the novel *The Long Firm*, describes with a relish not previously associated with menswear "a two-piece tonic mohair. Three buttoned single-breasted jacket, narrow lapels, flap pockets, from Harry Fenton's no doubt." Footballer and fashion icon George Best summed up men's attitudes in 1965: 'I used to wear very quiet clothes. Now, if I see something smart, no matter what anyone says, I buy it. I've got a black and white striped jacket. The lads in the team are always saying, "Here comes the butcher."' By the "Summer of Love" in 1967, men were dressing in Indian tops, protest T-shirts, brightly coloured satins, silks, and tapestry, and, with their long hair, boys and girls became increasingly indistinguishable.

← This long waistcoat from the famous London boutique Biba is in a rich, synthetic brocade fabric, and has a multitude of pockets. A trend for retro styles developed in menswear, popularizing waistcoats which were now sometimes worn unbuttoned and with jeans. Boutiques such as Biba and Bus Stop proliferated, making Kensington and Chelsea the centre of Swinging London. Anything by Biba is more valuable as a result of its origin, but the label continued long after the London store closed down and its founder, Barbara Hulanicki (b.1936), had left the company.

£60–80/$90–130   *Waistcoat*

← Compared with some examples from the 1960s, when stripes and multi-coloured patterns were fairly commonplace, these trousers are rather restrained. Turn-ups were banished, waists were low-cut, and "Chelsea boots" – ankle boots with elasticated sides, almost always in black – were now the norm, particularly after the Beatles were seen wearing them. Jeans retained their popularity, but were more flared than in the 1950s. The French firm, Le Cottier & Co., found success with "Long Line" slacks, licensed from Pierre Cardin, featuring wide belt-loops, a low, fitted waist, and no back pocket.

Trousers   **£50–80/$80–120**

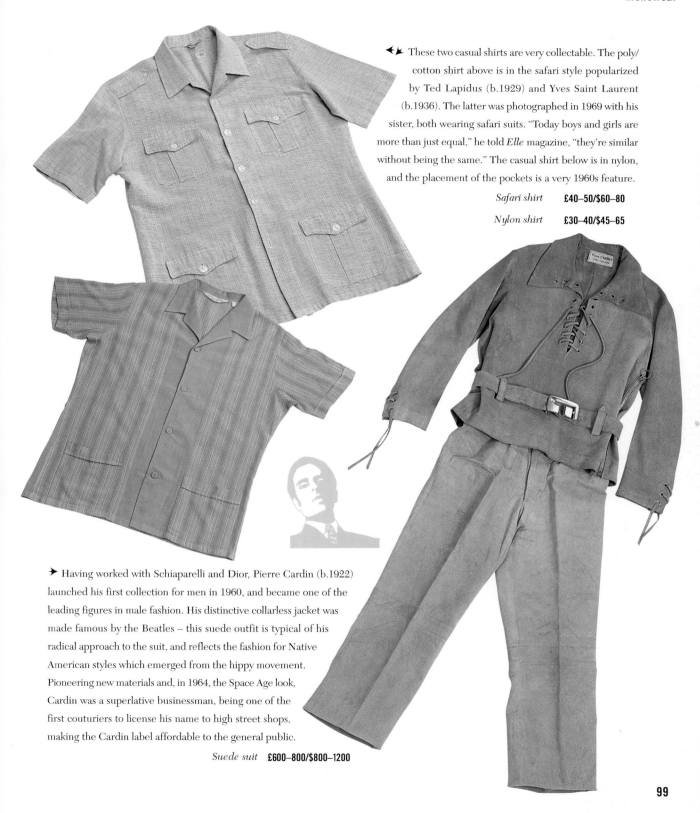

These two casual shirts are very collectable. The poly/cotton shirt above is in the safari style popularized by Ted Lapidus (b.1929) and Yves Saint Laurent (b.1936). The latter was photographed in 1969 with his sister, both wearing safari suits. "Today boys and girls are more than just equal," he told *Elle* magazine, "they're similar without being the same." The casual shirt below is in nylon, and the placement of the pockets is a very 1960s feature.

Safari shirt **£40–50/$60–80**
Nylon shirt **£30–40/$45–65**

Having worked with Schiaparelli and Dior, Pierre Cardin (b.1922) launched his first collection for men in 1960, and became one of the leading figures in male fashion. His distinctive collarless jacket was made famous by the Beatles – this suede outfit is typical of his radical approach to the suit, and reflects the fashion for Native American styles which emerged from the hippy movement. Pioneering new materials and, in 1964, the Space Age look, Cardin was a superlative businessman, being one of the first couturiers to license his name to high street shops, making the Cardin label affordable to the general public.

Suede suit **£600–800/$800–1200**

The Seventies

Known as "the decade that taste forgot", the 1970s were years of fashion extremes. Hot pants – tight shorts in eye-catching colours and fabrics – epitomized the limited impact of the Women's Liberation movement on fashion. Flares on trousers blossomed, and the floor-length maxi and calf-length midi arrived as alternatives to the ubiquitous mini-skirt. Denim was the fabric of the decade: brushed, patched, coloured, or flared, it was boosted by the new Unisex look and a vogue for dungarees. Victorian-style designs in natural fabrics made Laura Ashley the most popular British designer, and Japanese designers such as Kansai Yamamoto and Kenzo had a huge impact with clothes unfettered by references to traditional Western styling. But cut and finish were not important in the hippy movement – loose-fitting clothes were cheaply made in the Far East. Even this counter-culture sparked a reaction, being swept aside by the aggressive, sado-masochistic styles of punk and its high priestess, Vivienne Westwood.

Daywear

The dominance of street-led fashion continued to make manufacturers nervous about offering one definitive style for a season. The result was a glorious mixture of lengths and shapes, of revivals of past eras, of ethnic styles, of romanticism and of military chic. Second-hand and antique-looking clothes also became very fashionable. Barbara Hulanicki, at Biba, and Laura Ashley both offered fashion as lifestyle through their shops, while Calvin Klein (b.1942) and Ralph Lauren (b.1939) were the new ready-to-wear stars, and their separates were sold in chain stores throughout the USA. Influenced by Clare McCardell, Klein designed for a sporty figure: "If you are interested in clothes, then your body should be in shape." Women also loved Katherine Ross's costumes in *Butch Cassidy and the Sundance Kid*, snapping up Ralph Lauren's prairie-dress collection with its flounced white petticoats under denim skirts and broderie anglaise blouses. By the late 1970s punk rock had made ripped T-shirts, leather jackets, and safety pins fashionable, and Thierry Mugler, Jean-Paul Gaultier, and Vivienne Westwood were already shaping the next decade.

← Everyone wore waistcoats, in all colours and fabrics. This one is crocheted, a typical 1970s feature. The blouse is in polyester seersucker which, although it looked natural, washed and drip-dried easily. Such clothing was sold in separate areas for young women's fashions in department stores. These "shops within shops" looked different from the rest of the store, and soon opened up on their own on high streets: for instance Miss Selfridge was originally an off-shoot of the famous American-inspired store on London's Oxford Street, Selfridges.

Blouse   £40–50/$60–80

Waistcoat   £30–40/$40–60

▼ Despite the advance of the Green movement in the 1970s, synthetics were far from dead and buried, as shown by this classic "nice little blouse" in a polyester print. The puff sleeves are very romantic, in true 1970s style, but such blouses, with a large tie done up in a bow, became linked with Margaret Thatcher, the Conservative Party leader from 1975. Her look was devised by the advertising gurus Charles and Maurice Saatchi, who were her image consultants for her general election victory of 1979.

Blouse   £30–40/$40–60

← A Laura Ashley blouse with the "Peter Pan" collar, pin tucks, and frilly cuffs she made so popular. Laura Ashley (1925–85) started designing fabrics in the 1950s, but opened her first shop in 1968, and made the 1970s her decade. Made at a factory in Wales using natural fabrics, the styles harked back to Victorian and Edwardian times, conjuring up images of an idealized rural past. Among the most popular lines were full-length, pleated and lace-trimmed lawn nightdresses, and floral-sprigged, milk-maid-style maxi-dresses.

Blouse **£40–50/$60–80**

→ Skinny rib designs first came in during the 1960s, and cardigans in this style were popular as jackets from the early 1970s on. Ring-pulls were often used to highlight zip fastenings on jackets and catsuits. Knitwear came into its own as interest in ethnic styles continued to grow during the decade, and Patricia Roberts (b.1945) led fashions in hand-knitting with her 1930s-inspired styles, selling pattern books and Shetland style wool.

£40–50/$60–80 *Jacket*

← An extraordinarily 1920s-style design decorates this woman's shirt in a synthetic print. A revival of interest in the 1920s ran alongside numerous other revivals in the 1970s, and was marked by a taste for "Oxford bags", pullovers, and Fair Isle sweaters. The long, pointed collar on this shirt-style blouse is a characteristic 1970s feature, but spoon-shaped and tulip-shaped collars were also common.

£15–20/$25–35 *Blouse*

➤ The label, "Clothes by Samuel Sherman. Made in England", is in a style that reveals this wool jersey dress to be a 1970s garment. Paradoxically, protesters campaigning against American involvement in the war in Vietnam often wore army surplus clothes. Inevitably the military look was adapted for everyday wear, as features such as the pockets and the gilt-covered plastic buttons on this dress show.

Dress   **£80–120/$120–180**

✦ Tiered skirts were often home-sewn rather than commercially produced. This skirt, by Mushroom, is in viscose with broderie anglaise edging. Viscose was the basis for numerous items with an "urban peasant" look – it feels like a natural fabric, but is softer and crease-resistant.

£50–80/$80–120   *Tiered skirt*

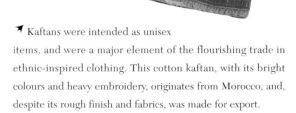

✦ Kaftans were intended as unisex items, and were a major element of the flourishing trade in ethnic-inspired clothing. This cotton kaftan, with its bright colours and heavy embroidery, originates from Morocco, and, despite its rough finish and fabrics, was made for export.

Kaftan   **£80–120/$120–180**

▼The spoon-shaped collar and button-down pockets on this woman's jacket were popular design features in the 1970s. Women wore jackets with skirts or trousers throughout the decade, but the fitted, matching suit was definitely out of fashion. Jackets such as this were worn long, but *Vogue* warned shorter women, "A jacket which comes well below the hip can make you look as if you are standing in a hole!"

£45–55/$70–90   *Jacket*

➤ Trouser suits were even more popular than in the 1960s, and Crimplene – a heat-treated polyester used here in a jersey fabric – was ideal for clear, sharp prints. Women who dressed in the latest fashions found that trousers that looked just like trousers were discouraged at traditional establishments, whatever the Paris fashion houses said. Wide-cut versions, including culottes, were more acceptable. The American designer Geoffrey Beene (b.1927) had enthusiastically promoted synthetic fibres in the early 1960s with the DuPont company, and his interest, coupled with his penchant for the easy lines of sportswear, helped spread the word for synthetics.

Trouser suit   £200–300/$300–500

Eveningwear

The "anything goes" styles of the daytime continued into the evening. Even when the mini was at its height in the 1960s, women still wore full-length dresses and skirts for formal evening occasions. In the era of the maxi and the midi, there was every reason for a varied approach to clothes for going out – evening trousers were considered especially smart. Adding to the confusion was the fact that women now wore day clothes as eveningwear, so formal lines were blurred to the point of obscurity. Part of the reason for this was economic: the oil crisis of the early 1970s had led to high inflation, and the end of the confident, carefree attitudes which had informed the forward-looking 1960s. People now bought their clothes more carefully: few now wanted eveningwear that would be unfashionable next year, so traditional styles held their own. The opportunities offered by new fabrics, however, proved a continuing source of fascination.

A typically romantic Ossie Clark blouse, this has full, turn-back cuffs and is in a combination of satin and polyester crêpe. Clark (1942–96) was extremely fond of crêpe and used it, along with satin, leather, jersey, and chiffon, in almost everything he made, from jackets to floor-length dresses. This blouse is clearly influenced by the Edwardian period, a theme which Clark developed explicitly in his collections in the early 1970s.

Ossie Clark blouse   **£300–400/$450–550**

A beautiful example of the ethnic influence adapted for Western tastes, with the typical 1970s halter neck. One ethnic group which attracted especial attention at this time was Native Americans, and their traditional beadwork and leather belts inspired fashions everywhere. This evening dress and cape are in a mixture of cotton and synthetic jersey, with punched and etched designs on the suede leather trim. Light-coloured, floor-length garments are often visibly stained around the hemlines, and it is fairly safe to assume that, if an item is offered to the collector in such a state, the stains are unlikely to come out even if further cleaning is attempted.

£150–200/$220–280   *Dress and cape*

◀ Conventional eveningwear such as the garment on the left enjoyed something of a revival in the 1970s, as maxi-length dresses could be worn at any time of the day. The satin dress on the right is by the London store Biba. Its cap sleeves and self-covered buttons have the look of the 1930s and 40s, but the cut of the skirt is clearly from the 1970s.

£100–150/$150–200   *Black dress*

£100–150/$150–200   *Red dress*

She's so swishy in her satin and tat, in her frock coat and bipperty bopperty hat . . .

From "Queen Bitch",
David Bowie, *Hunky Dory*, 1971

➤ This is a classic catsuit with its synthetic jersey material and leopard print. Catsuits in slinky fabrics such as Tricel and Dicel were popular, if somewhat daring, eveningwear in the 1970s. The British company Courtaulds produced synthetic fibres, having bought in 1904 the exclusive British rights to produce artificial silk. From 1914, it also produced nearly all the viscose yarn in Britain and the USA.

£80–120/$120–180   *Catsuit*

◀ This metallic, synthetic jersey dress is magnificent, and looks as if it might have been inspired by Marilyn Monroe and the pleated dress she wore in the 1950s film *Bus Stop*. Pleated materials lose their shape over time, and unfortunately pleats can be very difficult to restore. This affects the value of a garment, especially if, as in this example, it is dependent on those pleats being sharp to retain its shape and overall effect.

Pleated dress   £60–80/$80–120

Lingerie

Underwear was, by now, both lightweight and cheap to buy. The 1960s theme of following rather than shaping the figure continued, and roll-ons, the last stand of old-fashioned foundation wear, were banished to older generations of women. Even so, Playtex continued to advertise its girdles across the USA and Europe. Specialist corsetières finally disappeared from the High Street, although most towns had at least one shop which specialized in women's underwear for those who wanted a more personal or discreet service. Most women, especially younger ones now bought their underwear from department stores – in particular Marks & Spencer in Britain. The fashion for Russian and other ethnically-inspired designs popularized multi-layered and lace-edged petticoats under skirts, and Laura Ashley's retro style included Victorian-inspired petticoats and nightwear. But many more women now slept in big T-shirts, often depicting cuddly animals and cartoon characters.

◄ Bosoms were back in the 1970s, and this bra, with its stitching and the shaping in the cups, would make the most of the the wearer's natural curves. However, unlike the 1950s equivalent, it has no rigid shapings or stiffeners. Orange and purple are the two shades immediately associated with 1960s and 70s underwear, and brightly-coloured items like this are very typical – in reality few paid heed to the call made in the late 1960s to "Burn Your Bra".

£20–30/$30–50 *Orange bra*

◄ A classic and very pretty pair of 1970s cotton knickers, made in Italy by Primizia. Nylon underwear lost popularity as the decade progressed. An urban myth told of a woman who was injured, and embarrassed, when the static electricity generated by her nylon knickers caused an explosion! Synthetics did generate static, which caused garments to crackle and cling unnaturally to nylon slips, and cotton was generally more healthy next to the skin.

Knickers **£8–12/$12–18**

➤ ◄ New fabrics and styles are shown in these three contrasting bras. The strapless version, which is by Lady Silvet, has plenty of room for expansion as it is 25 per cent elastic. The white bra was made in the Philippines for Avon Fashions, a company much better known for its cosmetics. It is interesting because, with its seam-free cups, it is specially designed for wearing under a sweater. The dark pink bra is in a colour that is typical of the 1970s. Its label states that it was made in the USA, and is by the aptly-titled "Touch of Class Lacy plunge co-ordinates".

£15–20/$20–30	*Black bra*
£10–15/$15–20	*White bra*
£15–20/$20–30	*Pink bra*

◄ Women in the 1970s started to exercise to achieve the required silhouette. Fashionable centres such as Pineapple offered dance classes, and one major result of the fitness boom was the widespread popularity of dancers' clothes. Leotards and leg-warmers became everyday wear. Leg-warmers were pulled up to the thighs or, like this acrylic pair in a wonderful purple hue, worn baggy around the calves, adding to the warm, layered look. Socks also made a comeback. Long, coloured, woollen styles, and ankle-length socks in bright colours and eye-catching patterns were worn by all ages.

Ankle socks   **£5–8/$8–12**   *Leg-warmers*   **£8–12/$10–15**

Accessories

Accessories allowed designers to give full rein to the 1970s trend for hand-crafted items. This was in part a result of the revival of interest in the Arts and Crafts Movement, and especially in the designs of its leader, William Morris. It was also a reaction against the continued obsession with modernity and the Space Age – after all, men had landed on the Moon in 1969. The revival of home crafts meant that batik, tie-dyeing, and beaded or patchwork designs, whether home-made or mass-produced, were essentials. Accessories also had to be in proportion to the "Big Look" made popular by Japanese designers, with its oversized shirts, long skirts, and multiple layers of clothing. Platform boots, wedges, and stacked heels were teamed with floppy hats and large shoulder-bags. Trousers would be tucked into cowboy boots or worn with clogs. Handbags were larger as women carried more. Big coats were teamed with long scarves and matching hats and gloves, usually in wool. Jewellery was also long and drooping in the 1970s, preferably with an identifiably ethnic influence, usually Indian.

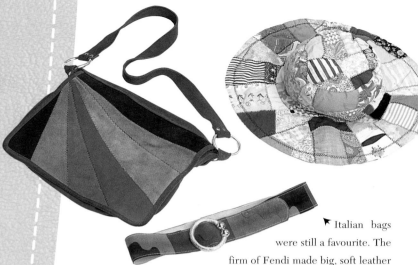

Italian bags were still a favourite. The firm of Fendi made big, soft leather bags – its patchwork suede ranges in particular were widely copied. The chrome rings on this example are also typical. Contrasting and fringed belts were worn with trousers, and often over loose tops – women tended to wear them with men's shirts. The patchwork hat is reversible. Patchwork was often used for clothing in the 1970s, especially for waistcoats, bags, and hats – Laura Ashley shops sold squares of her fabrics for the purpose.

Belt   **£8–12/$12–18**   *Bag*   **£25–35/$35–45**

Hat   **£12–18/$18–25**

The clutch bag was a 1970s constant, especially for occasions when spacious shoulder bags were too large. The ethnic influence is obvious in this example made of sisal, a fibre derived from agave, a Mexican plant with large, fleshy leaves. Also typical is the pink crochet hat, a common style which has remained popular. The other hat is in black plush fabric, with pink synthetic chenille edging and a petersham band, and would go best with satin or synthetic clothes.

Bag   **£20–30/$30–50**   *Pink crochet hat*   **£12–18/$18–25**

Black and pink hat   **£20–30/$30–50**

◄ Men and women wore huge platform soles, which were compulsory for the followers of "glam rock", and the pop star Elton John took the fashion to its jokey extreme. Retro styles in clothing created a demand for shoes to match, so women also wore Victorian-style lace-ups, albeit balanced on high 1970s heels. The men's leather platforms are labelled "The Shoe Place". Many shoe shops had a special cachet, but in Britain, Sacha produced among the most fashionable styles for the mass market, selling them through its own outlets.

Boots   **£60–80/$80–120**   *Shoes*   **£40–60/$60–80**

➤ Even sandals, like this green leather pair, were given platform soles and high heels. These 1940s-style shoes were made in Italy, and the label is "Creazione". Brown plastic platforms with large buckles appealed to younger women, and this style was made by "Fashion Eazies". Espadrilles had come a long way from their origins as rope-soled fishermen's shoes, and many had tapes rather than laces. Denim made frequent appearances on shoes, whether patched, dyed, embroidered, or, like this pair, as logos.

£40–50/$60–80   *Shoes*   **£60–80/$90–130**   *Sandals*

£40–50/$60–80   *Espadrilles*

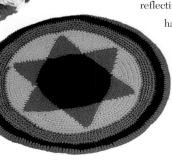

◄ The bright hat on the left is made from matching beer cans punched and crocheted together with nylon wool – a truly spectacular example of the obsession with crafts, and in very good condition! Labels and slogans were commonly used on accessories, reflecting the influence of the 1960s Pop Art of Andy Warhol. The crochet hat is in Rastafarian colours. The Rastafarian religion gained followers across the world – its best known adherent was Bob Marley, the Jamaican reggae singer. Crochet was an extremely popular craft in the 1970s, and everything, including dresses and bikinis, was crocheted with string, sequins, or more conventional yarns.

Beer-can hat   **£10–15/$15–20**   *Crochet hat*   **£10–15/$15–20**

Menswear

Flared trousers, wide collars, and long hair – permed or cut in the heavily layered "feather" style – were essential for the 1970s Man. In 1972, when Yves Saint Laurent cried "Down with the Ritz and up with the street!", he was referring to the way in which high fashion now took its inspiration from the street. The 1977 film *Saturday Night Fever* sparked a trend for the white suits and the slashed-to-the-waist, satin shirts of the typical "medallion" man. "Glam rock" was typified by David Bowie and Roxy Music, the latter adding a dash of the 1930s Lounge Lizard to their style. Soon even the most masculine of men occasionally wore a smear of eyeshadow, lip-gloss, and mascara. Wide, high-waisted trousers and long jackets with wide lapels and pointed cuffs went with high platforms, long sideburns, and droopy, "Zapata-style" moustaches. As the decade wore on, hippy-inspired fashions for Indian shirts and loon pants gave way to the harsher, radical demands of punk rock: leather motorcycle jackets, studs and chains, plastic bin-liners, and vinyl trousers – preferably with "bondage" straps – were the logical conclusion of this anti-fashion trend.

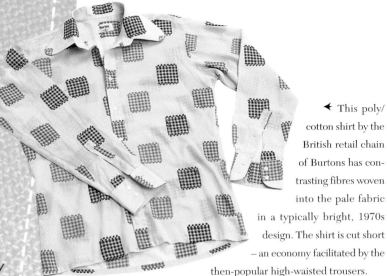

◄ This poly/cotton shirt by the British retail chain of Burtons has contrasting fibres woven into the pale fabric in a typically bright, 1970s design. The shirt is cut short – an economy facilitated by the then-popular high-waisted trousers.

Shirt   **£30–40/$45–55**

▼ A tribute to the "varsity" or "bomber" jacket, this reversible example reveals the continuing fascination with all-American styles. The colours, however, are emphatically 1970s, as is the "Glam" satin finish. Such jackets became known as "tour" jackets during the course of the decade, having been adopted as a uniform by rock stars and their groupies.

Jacket   **£100–150/$150–200**

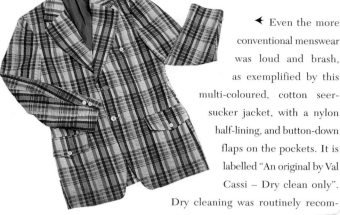

◄ Even the more conventional menswear was loud and brash, as exemplified by this multi-coloured, cotton seersucker jacket, with a nylon half-lining, and button-down flaps on the pockets. It is labelled "An original by Val Cassi – Dry clean only". Dry cleaning was routinely recommended, and is a good idea, especially where synthetic and natural fabrics are combined. However, in some cases, despite the labels, handwashing remained a far better and cheaper alternative.

Jacket   **£70–110/$100–150**

➤ This plush-denim suit is reminiscent of the type of outfit typically worn by young men dressing to impress. Made in viscose and polyester, it has the pointed cuffs and incredibly wide lapels that epitomized 1970s style. Such wide, flared trousers were usually complemented by high platforms, which prevented the wearer from tripping over swathes of fabric. Ties were no longer regarded as compulsory for men, who instead wore their collars splayed open, as on this poly/cotton shirt.

Suit   **£150–200/$220–280**   *Shirt*   **£30–40/$45–55**

◄ Although rock stars such as the New York Dolls and David Bowie encouraged more androgynous, even transvestite styles, men were generally less comfortable in kaftans than women. More often the move away from traditional masculine clothing was shown in the popularity of sleeveless jerkins and multi-coloured shirts. This jerkin is in suede leather and fastens with a belt. The Ben Sherman shirt has a motif based on the "England's Glory" matchbox label. Pop Art had a strong influence on fashion, and commercial trademarks and logos became increasingly popular as decorative motifs.

Jerkin   **£120–180/$180–220**   *Shirt*   **£60–80/$90–130**

Unisex

The trend for unisex clothing began in the 1960s, but only became widespread during the 1970s. Unisex fashions had been around in previous decades, but it was only now that men and women began wearing the same clothes bought from the same shops in large numbers. Unisex clothing meant men and women had a common approach to wearing what were essentially male fashions: jeans, jackets and knitwear, military chic, and fur coats. Despite the popularity of "glam rock", and Mick Jagger's famous appearance in a white dress at Brian Jones's memorial concert in Hyde Park, London, in 1969, very few men actually took to wearing women's garments. Kaftans were worn only by the most effete, such as Jason King, a character in the strangely popular British television series *Department S*. However, more decorative menswear did appeal to both sexes, and the popularity of "ethnic peasant" styles, which often featured more traditional unisex garments, further contributed to the growth of the unisex market.

◄ This wool waistcoat has a silk lining and synthetic braid. The label reads "Scott Lester Organization, Made in England". It is worn over a heavyweight-cotton patch shirt with brass buttons, made in Nepal for export under the label "Dispersion 59". Any garment made in India or Nepal had extra cachet in the 1970s – the cultures of these two countries were especially influential as a result of the streams of tourists from Western cultures who journeyed along the "Hippy Trail" through India to Katmandu.

Shirt	**£30–40/$45–55**
Waistcoat	**£20–30/$30–40**

◄ The ubiquitous Afghan coat was one of the most common of 1970s unisex fashions. The rough, embroidered goatskins, worn most often with jeans, were usually crudely made and cured, and tended to be rather smelly, so relatively few survive. The look was so popular that better-quality versions such as this, a Canadian sheepskin, also sold well. These "suburban" afghans retained the shaggy look, but were less pungent in wet weather!

Afghan coat **£220–280/$280–320**

➤ This patchwork cotton jacket and flared-collar shirt are a riot of 1970s influences: bright, clashing colours mixed with patch, button-down pockets. This jacket is in exceptionally good condition – when buying such items, the collector should pay attention to vulnerable areas. Worn elbows, sweat stains under the arms, and frayed buttonholes are difficult to repair or disguise, and so affect the value. The collar on the shirt is typically flared, and it should be worn with the top button undone.

Shirt   £15–20/$20–30   *Cotton patch jacket*   £50–60/$70–100

➤ Tank tops were the unisex version of pullovers, and horizontal stripes in contrasting or even clashing colours were especially popular. All three are in acrylic, a synthetic wool substitute developed in 1947. The lime green and mauve version is by Skylar, which was a popular brand of the time, as was Pippa Dee, the brand of the maroon and white style.

Tank tops (each)   £18–24/$24–32

➤ Levis retained their popularity as the coolest jeans on the planet, but nothing was more uncool than an obviously new pair of jeans, so manufacturers, including Levi Strauss & Co., began producing denim that looked old. These are obviously from the 1970s because of the wide flare from the knee. Trousers with this leg shape were known as "loons".

£30–40/$45–55   *Patch Levis*

The Eighties

Fashion influences at the start of the 1980s were diverse, but old-fashioned royalty and the "New Romantic" bands were prominent. Lady Diana Spencer, the future Princess of Wales, favoured floaty, flowery dresses in demure prints, choosing David and Elizabeth Emanuel to design her wedding dress in 1982. Meanwhile the combination of punk and New Romanticism encouraged many designers to break rules – fabrics such as rubber and vinyl, more fetish than fashion, prevailed. Designers worked with pop bands, and the growth of the music video encouraged crossovers between style, fashion, and music. Jean-Paul Gaultier was the best showman, whether being refused entry at the Cannes film festival for being improperly dressed in a jacket and shorts suit, or refashioning corsets as outerwear, notably for pop star Madonna. Japanese designers consolidated their influence, dominating the Paris collections of the early 1980s with their draped, unstructured clothing. The aggressive politics of Margaret Thatcher helped to establish the power suit, in which all but the tallest women looked like boxes, and Nancy Reagan, wife of President Ronald Reagan, revived the sheath dress – ostentation was back.

Daywear

The 1980s saw an extraordinary mish-mash of styles and fabrics. Statements came to the fore, and in this context it makes sense that *Vogue* thought Margaret Thatcher, with her suits and floppy-bowed blouses, a fashion trendsetter. Legislation aimed at ensuring equal pay and outlawing sex discrimination began to have an impact, and career women wanted smart and practical clothes – the power suit, with its shorter skirt and enormous shoulder pads, came into its own. Greater spending power also meant that some could now buy designer clothes off the peg. Work was not the only focus: a new breed of young designers, especially those from St Martin's School of Art in London, adopted a vibrant and questioning approach which mirrored the 1960s. Puff-ball, crinoline, and ra-ra skirts flourished briefly on the High Street – this fixes them in a specific time, making them desirable, if far from wearable, for the collector.

◄ One of a number of British design teams that came to the fore in the 1980s, Body Map was formed in 1982 by David Holah (b.1958) and Stevie Stewart (b.1958). A preoccupation with unstructured layers defined their unique approach, and their combinations of fabrics, seen here in the lace trim on this heavy-weight wool jacket, was often surprising.

£100–150/$150–200   *Body Map jacket (some damage)*

◄ In the 1970s the fascination with a range of different styles had led people in many different directions. In the 1980s, as this polyester dress with a satin finish per-fectly demonstrates, those contrasting influences were often combined in the same garment, with varying degrees of success. This dress tries to be feminine and Oriental, but also has military-style epaulettes. The overly eclectic approach is best summed up by the scarlet chrysanthemum embroi-dered on the cerise background.

Dress   £25–35/$40–50

➤ An example of the required style at conventional weddings in the 1980s. This imitation silk suit might also be worn with a little pill-box hat in matching fabric. It is more valuable because of its provenance: it was made by Hilary Boulton for the 1987 film *Personal Services*. The foam-plastic shoulder pads are massive, and the peplum is stiffened with black net.

Suit and hat **£120–180/$180–220**

➤ The styling of this jacket is characteristic of the 1980s: longer length jackets with three-quarter or rolled-up sleeves were part of a trend which also influenced men's fashions. In addition, acetate was a very common and versatile fabric, especially in metallic-type finishes, and jackets of this type were a regular sight on high streets.

£15–20/$20–30 *Jacket*

➤ A designer who was never part of the mainstream, Jean Muir (1933–95) was fascinated by the way fabrics could be cut and manipulated to achieve the disciplined fluidity which was her trademark. It is only when her clothes are put on that one can understand what she was aiming for. Her styles are classics so women keep them for ever, which makes them difficult for the collector to find.

£300–400/$450–550 *Jean Muir dress*

➤ Liza Bruce (b.1955) is an American designer who first came to attention in the 1980s, when her swimwear became famous as much for its incredible prices as its innovative designs. She broadened her range throughout the decade, taking a lead designing outfits for the by-now ubiquitous aerobics classes, and the videos that followed in which ladies "glowed" but never sweated.

Leotard and leggings   £50–80/$80–120

◂ Culottes – trousers cut very full to look like a skirt – enjoyed a revival. This culotte dress, in a cotton/polyester print with a jersey bodice, has self-covered buttons, and the culottes are cut with a panel at the front to make an even fuller skirt than usual. The term "culotte" comes from the French word for knee breeches.

Culotte dress   £40–50/$60–80

➤ Almost a 1930s beachwear set in its styling, or even a 1960s mini-outfit, this ensemble could be worn nightclubbing or during the daytime. Cropped tops extended their popularity to most age groups during the 1990s, but their success first began with garments like these. This set is complete with its original contrast-ing buttons, which adds to its value.

Shorts set   £30–40/$50–80

➤ John Galliano (b.1960) was another of the young British designers to make his name, almost on graduation, in the 1980s. He combines a strong sense of history with a taste for the absurd, and this beautiful jacket is typical of his brand of eccentricity. The collar, in a single shape, can be worn on the shoulders, as shown, or pulled up over the head like a traditional monk's cowl. Any item from the early part of an established designer's career is likely to be collectable. This jacket is also more valuable because it is so distinctive.

Jacket   **£450–550/$700–1000**

➤ Leggings became mainstream in the 1980s. Women found them comfortable and easy to wash and wear, so took to them enthusiastically. Supermodels, traditionally tall and thin, could look very good in these hip-hugging, unforgiving garments, but most women found they emphasized bottoms and tummies. This pair is a classic of the genre. In synthetic jersey and with a leopard print, they are no more suitable for aerobics than the non-matching print top.

£20–30/$30–40   *Leggings*   **£15–20/$20–30**   *Top*

Eveningwear

If the prevailing right-wing political climate in the 1980s informed an aggressively glitzy approach to fashion, eveningwear took the trend to the extreme. The actress Joan Collins played the poisonous Alexis in *Dynasty*, the American drama about rich people who were as miserable as they were wealthy. The flamboyant costumes on both *Dynasty,* and rival show *Dallas*, sparked a demand for cocktail wear including little silk suits, and jewelled dresses with pinched waists, flared peplums, and ludicrously over-padded shoulders. Some of the most opulent eveningwear came from Oscar de la Renta (b.1932), Bill Blass (1922–2002), Emanuel Ungaro (b.1933), and Karl Lagerfeld (b.1938), the latter now designing for Chanel. By 1986, however, this trend had largely dissipated. Across Europe, despite the illusion of wealth, unemployment broke all records, and dissent was growing. The backlash against ostentatious wealth, itself a reaction to the anti-materialistic values of hippy trendsetters, called for dressing down in eveningwear as well as daywear. John Galliano, arch as ever, took up this theme in 1986, with an empire-line evening dress in cheesecloth.

➤ Suitable, like much of women's clothing during the decade, for evening or daywear, this jacket, with the label "Hily Misawe", is a must for the 1980s fashion collector. The high, straight back is in a white viscose moiré, and the jacket is trimmed with stiff, black moiré ruffles that feel almost like plastic.

Jacket   **£100–150/$150–200**

➤ Another daytime and evening dress. The asymmetrical "wing" on the front is a definite 1980s feature – post-modernism was all the rage – and shades of purple and mauve were also widely used. This is the sort of dress worn, with white stiletto-heeled shoes, by what the British tabloid newspapers, then at the height of their popularity, labelled the "Essex Girl": Essex was populated during the 1950s and 60s by working-class Londoners, many of them moving out from the East End.

£40–60/$60–80

Mini-dress

➤ Thierry Mugler's (b.1948) influences are from the 1940s and 1950s, as this dress, with its asymmetrical skirt emphasizing the hips, shows. Despite that, its short length and metal buckle make it distinctively 1980s. Mugler often takes the lines of his clothes from earlier decades, and exaggerates shoulders, waists, and necklines in a theatrical way that points to his early training as a dancer.

£400–500/$600–800   *Dress*

➤ Japanese designers continued to exert a powerful influence. Their fondness for draping and flowing materials, and the sculpted look of their clothes, have had an enormous impact. This cheesecloth evening dress by Issey Miyake (b.1935) is uncompromising in its style. Miyake is fascinated by body sculpture – so much so that in the 1980s he produced items such as a bustier in moulded plastic and a bamboo breastplate.

Cheesecloth dress   **£150–200/$220–280**

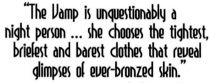

"The Vamp is unquestionably a night person ... she chooses the tightest, briefest and barest clothes that reveal glimpses of ever-bronzed skin."
From *Even More Dash Than Cash*
by Kate Hogg (Vogue/Century 1989)

➤ Softer styles were also available, and this purple garment, made in England for John Marks is a good example. From the collector's point of view, the label is interesting because it includes British, American, and European sizes. This dress is in the material Banlon, a version of nylon which is a registered trademark of Joseph Bancroft and Sons of the USA, as is the design of a cat sitting on a cushion. Labels do not necessarily add value to a piece, but they add interest, and can also extend our knowledge, especially when trying to date a garment.

£80–120/$120–180   *Purple dress*

Lingerie

Variety was the theme of 1980s lingerie. Tights had dominated the hosiery market in the early 1970s, but, after little more than ten years, stockings were back. The New Romantics, shortly followed by the Goths, inspired underwear design, and the pop star Madonna in particular helped to popularize the idea of underwear as outerwear – although Jean-Paul Gaultier did not design the trademark gold bustier until the early 1990s. On high streets and in railway stations, chains of shops such as Sock Shop and Knickerbox sold ranges of stockings in bright colours, exaggerated patterns, and sparkling fabrics. Seamed stockings were in demand, and the Princess of Wales further encouraged the romantic theme with her penchant for tights and shoes with bows at the ankles. Silk was the preferred fabric in knickers and tops, and French knickers, camisoles, and teddies, all unseen since the 1950s, were newly fashionable. Underwear no longer moulded the body to the desired shape – in theory at least, women were supposed to achieve the required forms through exercise.

◄ These two camisole tops, one in peach polyester and the other in black façonné silk, were sold as separates, and the full range of suspender belts, French knickers, and briefs was also usually available as separates. 1980s camisoles differ from earlier equivalents in a number of ways, most obviously in the fabrics and labels – washing instructions which warn about tumble drying, for example, only appeared in the 1980s. Although collectable, they have little financial value as yet but are worth putting aside, especially in a full set of knickers, top, and suspenders.

Black silk camisole   **£10–20/$15–25**   *Peach camisole*   **£10–15/$15–20**

◄ These horizontally striped tights were sold by Sock Shop in a wide range of colour combinations. The black tights have a gilt tiger motif – a classic 1980s touch. Designer label stockings and tights in outrageous colours were very popular, and any colour or combination was acceptable, apart from tan and flesh shades. Christian Dior was selling very expensive hosiery under his own label in the 1950s, but the sale of designer merchandise on the High Street only really began to take off in the course of the 1980s.

£5–10/$8–12   *Stockings*

£3–5/$5–8   *Tights*

◄ Thermal underwear had been around for years, but it was only now that it became of mainstream interest. Damart was the most popular make – a mail order company for woolly underwear which belatedly attained fashionable status. Thermal vests are so called because of the manufacturing process which traps air in tiny pockets in the fabric, giving extra warmth. This one by Marks & Spencer might be worn underneath or as a top.

£8–12/$12–15 *Thermal vest*

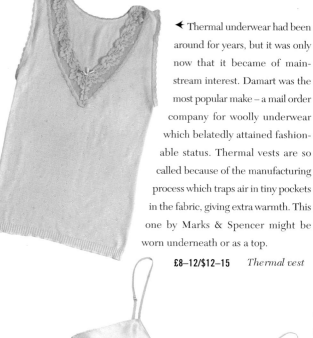

▲ Many leading designers in the 1980s created ranges of underwear, and most produced versions of bustiers. Just as in the 1950s, these new styles were often exotically embroidered. The black satin version here has elaborate ruching, while the gold and black example is by Charnos. Founded in the 1930s, Charnos originally made stockings but expanded very successfully in the 1950s to produce lingerie.

Gold bustier **£20–25/$30–40** *Black bustier* **£15–20/$25–35**

◄ The trend to prettier, frillier underwear, such as this polyester teddy, owed much to Janet Reger (b.1935), the British designer famous since the 1960s for her glamorous and expensive lingerie. The business failed and was bought by Berlei, but Janet Reger still designs under her own name – any item with her label is worth more as a result. The teddy style has its origins in the 1920s, but this 1980s version is made of satin polyester and fastens with plastic poppers.

£15–20/$20–30 *Teddy*

◤ These silk French knickers are machine embroidered. The high-cut leg was a feature of 1980s French knickers – in earlier decades square-cut legs had been preferred. At the same time, cotton and cotton-mixture knickers were making a comeback, in bikini, garter, and g-string shapes.

£8–12/$12–18 *Silk French knickers*

Accessories

Designer labels flooded the high street in the 1980s – if you could not afford a Chanel suit, at least you could afford a Hermès headscarf. The logos of the leading fashion houses were incorporated into innumerable accessories, and, aided by the political atmosphere in both America and Britain, ostentation and obvious wealth became fashionable. Accessories had to be eye-catching – flashy jewellery was a common sight on the brash power suits of the day. Paralleling the return of unashamed luxury, the street styles of the Goths and New Romantics encouraged lace gloves, heavy jewellery, and eye make-up. Across most styles, hair was more prominent than in the 1970s: lacquers of varying strengths, styling gels, mousses, and spray-in colours all combined to create the "big hair" look that everyone was trying to achieve.

↑ Belts were an inevitable feature in the 1980s – a tightly drawn or empha-sized waist highlighted widely padded shoulders and exaggerated hips. These two are, for different reasons, typical, and therefore espe-cially collectable: the leaf-motif version is in gilt, which was acceptable in the 1980s for daywear as well as eveningwear. The wide black version is Italian. Styling in Italy made leaps forward during the decade, and, as always, the country's leather goods led the way.

£8–12/$12–18   *Gold belt*   £15–20/$20–30   *Black leather belt*

↓ ↖ Clutch bags, shoulder bags, and anything in between were accept-able in the 1980s. The trend towards larger bags had started in the previous decade, and this gold version labelled "Suzi Smith" is in the same tradition, but has the gold shoulder strap that was so popular in the 1980s. Padding is another common feature of the decade that the collector should look out for, most famously manifested in the ubiquitous shoulder pad, and it features on the shell-shaped, blue leather clutch bag.

Gold shoulder bag   £15–20/$20–30

Clutch bag   £12–15/$15–20

➤ Vivienne Westwood (b. 1941) continued to shock and innovate in the 1980s, and these magnificent boots show why – like most of her ideas, this style has subsequently been widely copied. At the beginning of the decade her interest shifted from punks and bondage to New Romantic fashions – she gave titles such as "Pirates" and "Savages" to her 1980s collections. Any collector specializing in Vivienne Westwood, or in the latter half of the 20th century, would want to feature something from each phase of her career.

Boots   **£700–1000/$1000–1500**

➤➤ Trainers became fashion items in their own right, moving beyond the sports fields. Puma, and in particular Adidas, a German make whose name derived from the manufacturer's name, Adi Dassler, were both among the names with particular clout in the late 1970s and early 1980s. As the decade progressed, Reebok and Nike acquired a similar cachet, and new styles developed with more padding around the tongue and higher, built-up soles. Both these pairs are from the early 1980s: the Adidas pair are in the leather "Record" style, and the red nylon pair, by Puma, were made in Canada.

Adidas trainers   **£30–40/$45–55**

Puma trainers   **£30–40/$45–55**

Menswear

Power dressing was, in the 1980s, the key for men too. The "Yuppie" (short for Young Upwardly-mobile Professional) was someone with a highly paid job in the financial sector, a dog-eat-dog attitude, and a taste for champagne. In the film *Wall Street* Michael Douglas's character, Gordon Gekko, exemplified the archetypal yuppie with his sharp suit and brightly coloured braces. In more relaxed environments, men wore Chino trousers, based on US Army fatigues, polo shirts, and smart shirts more sober in styling than the flamboyant designs of the 1970s. Homosexuality was no longer completely taboo, and gay culture influenced fashion at all levels. Some gay men adopted the "Clone" style – moustaches, white T-shirts, and black leather jackets. Some shaved their heads and even wore Nazi regalia, deliberately imitating homophobic neo-Nazi thugs, seizing the imagery as a sign of gay oppression. Dedicated followers of fashion bought style bibles *The Face* and *i-D*. In 1984, a male correspondent wrote, "I consider myself typical of your readership ... I'm a quite well educated, middle-class unemployed trendy who is quite partial to wearing tight black jeans and pointed suede shoes with a sprinkling of diamanté."

✖ Tailored in England for "The Special Branch Clothing Company", this jacket is in viscose and polyester with a polyester lining. Alongside the sharp suits, men adopted a studied casual look with jackets like this, which, despite their often totally synthetic composition, looked like linen or cotton and were frequently worn with the sleeves pushed or rolled up.

£40–50/$60–80

Jacket

◀ A magnificent example of the growing fashion for PVC, leather, and rubber clothing, inspired by street styles, which continued unabated throughout the 1990s. This pair, made in England, is washable but carries on its label the surely unnecessary warning "Do Not Iron".

Vinyl trousers   **£50–80/$80–120**

The aggressive wealth of 1980s style made eye-catching waistcoats inevitable. These two collarless examples both typify their period. The upper one is in brocade and the lower in a leopard-skin print that is barely intended to resemble fur. Generally waistcoats like this are quite easy to find because they soon look dated and are put at the back of the wardrobe. In addition, they do not command particularly high prices because they rarely wore out, so there are many still around.

Brocade waistcoat **£15–20/$20–30**   *Leopard waistcoat* **£15–20/$20–30**

Giorgio Armani (b.1934) was probably the most influential menswear designer of the late 20th century. This polyester suit, with its sharp lapels and roomy 1980s cut, is typical of the period, but not, however, of Armani's work: his designs are usually softer, and use natural fabrics. He set the scene for the decade with his highly stylized Emporio Armani shops, which opened in the more up-market parts of the world's major cities. A feature of this suit is a double rubber band on the inside of the trousers, which holds the shirt in place and is definitely more acceptable than tucking it into one's underpants!

Armani suit **£300–400/$450–550**

Unisex

By 1985 the death of "Yuppie" style was being regularly foretold, often with some relish. A "New Seriousness" was heralded in the *Guardian* in 1985, with "the swing back to architecture and design ... and the post-*Witness* fad for the Amish look" together with the revelation that "teenagers ... don't want fashion pages". Clubland had begun to influence mainstream clothes, as had gay culture, especially through pop stars such as Boy George of Culture Club, whose style of dress was copied by fans of both sexes. Anti-nuclear protesters also provoked styles, helping to originate a fashion for women wearing Doctor ("Doc.") Marten's boots and shoes. The designer Katherine Hamnett (b.1947) made her point to Margaret Thatcher at a Downing Street reception with her T-shirt which proclaimed the anti-nuclear message, "58 per cent don't want Cruise." Sportswear as daywear also came to the fore, most notably in the much-despised shell-suit – an essential item for any comprehensive collection of 1980s fashion!

◄ This T-shirt has a wonderful punk feel to it. The idea of letters and images cut from newspapers has its origins in the Sex Pistols' first album, *Never Mind the Bollocks, Here's the Sex Pistols*. Punk sought to shock by juxtaposing soft, non-threatening images such as toys or animals with an aggressive treatment such as this crude-cut, graffiti-like design. So much of punk styling set trends that early items already command high prices, particularly for the work of recognized designers.

T-shirt   £20–30/$30–50

◄ Popular with bikers since Marlon Brando and Lee Marvin wore them in the classic 1950s film *The Wild One*, leather biker jackets became very much part of mainstream fashion for both men and women during the 1980s, particularly as leather, like rubber and PVC, became more widely used in all types of garments. This American-made version of the classic remains in extremely good condition.

Leather jacket   £50–60/$70–110

Tim Burton's 1989 film *Batman* restored the caped crusader to his original comic-strip context of Gothic ambivalence. Merchandising around films has been with us since the days of silent films, and this T-shirt will appeal to collectors of film memorabilia as well as comic-book fans, all of which increases the value. The rubber T-shirt, to be worn with leather or PVC trousers, was the coolest and hottest style statement. This T-shirt is in very good condition: rubber perishes if not oiled lightly, and a dusting of talcum powder has been used to prevent the two halves from sticking together.

£40–50/$60–80   *Rubber T-shirt*

Batman T-shirt

If aerobics marked the start of the fitness boom in the 1970s, skiing was the 1980s alternative, as cheaper travel made winter holidays possible. Ski-wear in bright colours and new, lightweight fabrics was essential for fashionable appeal as well as practicality. The jacket's padding, and the contrasting colours, make this a very good example of 1980s ski-wear. The tracksuit-style top is by Nike, a leading fashion sportswear brand in the 1980s and 90s. Nike garments, especially trainers, are worth more because of the name. The colour combination, like that of the ski jacket, is very distinctive of the decade.

£40–50/$60–80   *Nike jacket*   **£30–40/$45–55**   *Ski jacket*

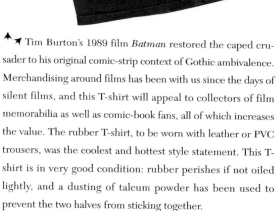

The Nineties

Diana, Princess of Wales, still reflected and defined the look for many fashion fanatics. Her personal style had changed markedly since the early 1980s, and her patronage of Catherine Walker, Bruce Oldfield, and Gianni Versace pointed to a highly sophisticated approach, with the occasional nod – via Versace – to vulgar show. Fashion houses mourned her death in 1997, dressing the windows of salons near her London home with white lilies and black cloth. In the early 1990s grunge was the anti-fashion statement, epitomized by mismatched, torn, ill-fitting, and dirty clothes, usually second-hand – it was the chosen style of "Generation X" in America, and in Britain was strongly linked to the New Age Traveller movement. However, designer labels tightened their grip on the fashion-conscious: Westwood, Versace, Galliano and Prada were among the most sought-after names. A new generation of super-models such as Kate Moss and Naomi Campbell became as famous as pop stars, while gossip magazines fuelled the fashion for celebrity frock-watching. The Spice Girls boosted demand for tiny mini-skirts, midriff-revealing tops, low-slung combat trousers, and towering platform trainers – the uniform of "Girl Power".

Daywear

"Cool Brittania" became one of the catch-phrases of the decade, and British designers Alexander McQueen, Stella McCartney, and John Galliano lead the way in Paris. Italian style ranged from the extravagance of Versace to the elegance of Prada, whilst Grunge made anti-fashion fashionable. Each new design was instantly copied by high street stores – micro-minis, long, trailing, floral skirts, animal prints, and smart business suits all had their day. Young people adopted cargo pants for casual wear, and traditional jeans became a middle-aged fashion, unless customised, Gucci-style, with feathers and appliqué. The entire 20th century was pillaged for its fashions by designers: 1920s slip dresses, 1950s beaded cardigans, and the whole of the 1970s look were revived. In Vogue?sDecember 1999 issue, combining the old with the new was recommended – the wearable collectables of the new millennium would be "classic items or old pieces of clothing from famous designers".

◄ This Voyage top would be suitable for day or eveningwear. The name Voyage conjures up soft, beautifully made garments with velvet trimmings, as in this collar, and the trademark fastening. The company itself markets and advertises little, but its name has become known through the label's popularity with film stars and other fashion icons of the 1990s. As one of the more innovative and interesting labels to emerge during the decade, Voyage is well worth collecting.

£75–90/$110–135   *Voyage top*

◄ Diesel is an Italian company, but it is best known for a look based on American working clothes from the 1950s, emphasized with advertising which uses period styling and colours. This no-nonsense polyester jacket is typical. Although Diesel aimed to bring an Italian interpretation of a particular element in American clothing to the wider world, its main market has been in the USA, where it has been phenomenally successful.

Diesel jacket   £30–40/$45–55

➤ This jacket is part of a wool suit, which also has a matching fur muff. It was designed by Thomas von Nordheim (b.1969), a German designer based in London. He is strongly influenced by the shapes and cut of 1940s clothes, and uses well-cut fabrics, trimmed with custom-made buttons and, as in this collar, dyed fox fur. His eveningwear, which often features rich brocades and silks, is particularly spectacular.

£2000–3000/$3000–4000 *Suit*

▲ Alexander McQueen (1969–2012) was one of the most successful designers of the 1990s. From his early training, at a tailor in London's Savile Row, he was fascinated by the way clothes can accentuate the shapes of the body – most famously in his "bumster" trousers of the mid-1990s, the first of his many designs which aimed to shock. In 1996 he became head of design at the Paris house of Givenchy. This sweater, in angora and nylon, was made in Italy.

£200–300/$300–400 *Sweater*

➤ Vivienne Westwood has said that the only ideas worth following are those that shock, but a strong sense of history also informs her clothes. Starting out in London's King's Road in the 1970s, she became known for her punk fashions which made much use of rubber and leather, with fetishistic styling. Her designs over the years have featured references to Elizabethan and Georgian dress, and this suit has the sharp edges and shape of classic Westwood design.

£300–500/$450–650 *Suit*

➤ A beautiful dress by the hugely successful Agnès B, in a length typical of the 1990s. Agnès B was born Agnès Troublé in 1941, and many of her early designs in the 1970s were adapted from French uniforms, an enduring source of inspiration for designers in France since the 1950s. This dress is a polyester print and has two large patch pockets.

Dress **£40–50/$60–80**

◄ Mini-skirts had never quite gone out of fashion since their arrival in the 1960s, but the version for the 1990s was very, very short. Lycra and other stretchy fabrics were especially well suited to this brief style. This example, by Quontum, a company based in Brighton, England, is in purple suede. Leather and other skins reasserted themselves, helped by the continued popularity of Italian designers, who have generally favoured such materials. By the end of the decade, zebra print, in synthetic and brushed finishes, was as popular as the ubiquitous leopard pattern.

£20–30/$30–50 *Skirt*

◄ Indicative of the late 20th-century fascination with retro styles, wide trousers such as these clearly draw on styles popular in the 1970s. This pair in a synthetic print material is by Dolce & Gabbana, a company founded by Domenico Dolce (b.1958) and Stefano Gabbana (b.1962) in 1982. They became famous in the 1990s when the pop star Madonna wore their widely copied rhinestone-covered bodice.

£100–150/$150–200 *Trousers*

➤ Comme des Garçons was founded in 1969 by Japanese designer Rei Kawakubo (b.1942). She, like many contemporaries, took the humble T-shirt, revitalizing it as a designer garment. The range of ideas and fabrics applied to T-shirts in the 1990s was astonishing. Kawakubo became known for flouting traditional ideas about body shapes – this T-shirt continues the theme, seeming badly cut.

T-shirt　　**£50–80/$80–120**

◄ This silk print dress with a rayon lining is by Versace, the immensely successful Italian company which produced daring designs emphasizing fluidity and bold colours. Versace made an impact on the fashion scene in Britain when the actress Elizabeth Hurley appeared in newspapers in an evening dress apparently held together with strategically placed rows of safety pins. On the death of the founder Gianni (1946–97) in 1997, his sister Donatella continued the distinctive Versace style.

£250–350/$400–500　*Dress*

➤ Franco Moschino (1950–1994), who established another internationally renowned Italian firm, worked with Versace, but his use of visual puns suggests that he should be considered as the heir to Schiaparelli. This pair of leggings in cotton and elastane is a classic, with its comment "Oh no, not another silly Moschino print!!..." Moschino first achieved fame in the 1980s for his belts and bags featuring the name Moschino in large gilt letters.

Leggings (damaged)　　**£40–50/$60–80**

Eveningwear

Eveningwear in the 1990s provided a succinct summary of the general ambivalence of the time. Jokey garments, the "little girl lost" look, and the power-dressed woman in Prada's and Donna Karan's severe and serious lines, were all equally popular. People spent more money on going out than in the previous decade. Theatre and cinema audiences increased, and whatever else the dawn of the next millennium symbolized, it certainly meant a party to most people. Glamour was back in style, and as ever film stars and models were to the fore in promoting fashions, dressing up for premières or at restaurants where the paparazzi gathered to photograph them. A new generation of "It Girls" from wealthy families achieved fame merely by being seen wearing the right dress at the right party, and were courted by designers for their patronage. The cult of celebrity was epitomized by Sotheby's auction of Geri Halliwell's frocks, where collectors competed for the Union Jack mini-dress worn by "Ginger Spice", which was one of the most famous evening dresses of the decade.

◄ This Clements Ribiero dress is in silk, rayon, and polyester, with a separate nylon lining. Clements Ribiero is a husband and wife team consisting of English designer Suzanne Clements (b.1968) and Brazilian designer Inacio Ribiero (b.1963), who studied at St Martin's School of Art, London, in 1991. This is a beautiful example of their work, with the delicate flower motifs picked out in metallic thread. The square-necked nylon lining peeping above the V-neck of the dress is a characteristic 1990s feature.

£150–200/$200–300   *Flower dress*

◄ The little black dress thrived in the 1990s, here in a severe version by Prada in rayon and Spandex. The firm of Prada, founded in Italy in 1913, made exclusive leather goods until Miuccia Prada (b.1949) took over in the late 1970s, hitting the headlines with an iconographic nylon backpack. Prada's first ready to wear collection was launched in 1988, and Prada has become one of the leading fashion names of the 1990s – film stars Nicole Kidman and Uma Thurman have both worn Prada to Academy Awards ceremonies – so the label is well worth collecting now.

£200–300/$300–400

Black dress

◄ Founded in Italy in the 1960s, the family firm of Benetton initially sold knitwear. It now has branches all over the world, and is famous for its controversial advertising campaigns. Its distinctive shops feature garments stacked in contrasting or toning colours, and this nylon top, with its bright colours and shaggy texture, is typical of its simple but challenging approach.

£25–35/$40–50 *Benetton top*

➤ Fishtail dresses underwent a brief revival, and this one, by Sergio, gives a good idea of their appeal. The 1990s versions had very, very low-cut backs, sometimes revealing the cleavage known colloquially as the "builder's bum" after the effect of loose-fitting jeans on many male builders. Fishtail dresses are not especially collectable, but they can be fun to wear.

£50–60/$80–120 *Fishtail dress*

◄ This long dress is by Red or Dead, and accurately sums up the "post-modernist irony" of the period: long, formal eveningwear in velvet could still have a fun theme such as these footprints. Red or Dead is a British firm, part of the eccentric, trend-setting wave of British designers whose work was so influential throughout the 1980s and 1990s.

Dress **£60–80/$80–120**

Lingerie

Underwear, as ever, reflected the lives of the women who wore it. The fitness boom, which started in the 1970s, coupled with the increasing demands women made of underwear in their more active lifestyles, meant that by the 1990s women wanted underwear that enhanced, rather than controlled, their figures. Health was also a consideration: cotton-based mixtures in briefs were thought more healthy, and fears, especially in the USA, about the risk of silicone breast implants encouraged sales of Wonderbras as an alternative to surgery. Stockings continued to be popular, and traditional fastenings with suspenders were also considered more healthy and attractive than tights or elastic-topped hold-ups. Lycra, elastane, and spandex all meant that underwear fitted the individual form far more easily than before. Even so, specialist and larger underwear shops introduced measuring services, as women were no longer used to making sure their underwear fitted – a far cry from the days of the corsetières a hundred years before!

◄ Two magnificent sports bras which, contrasted with the bras opposite, show how varied the silhouette of the 1990s female had become. These two bras are in totally synthetic materials and are designed to fit closely to the body. The fabric is elasticated, so there is little chance of the straps slipping down or the main part riding up. The bright red colour shows how far the "underwear as outerwear" style had progressed by the end of the century – women could wear bras like this without covering tops.

£20–30/$30–40   *Sports bras (each)*

◄ A short, synthetic nightdress, "Salon Rose", by Marks & Spencer, this style, in short and full-length versions, was one of the hottest sellers in Marks & Spencer at the end of 1999. The retail chain had suffered a downturn in the late 1990s as women, most of whom had routinely shopped for their lingerie at "M & S", found other sources for their day-to-day underwear. It tried to regain ground with new lines by fashionable designers such as Agent Provocateur, famous for their sexy lingerie, and with a more glamorous approach.

Nightdress   £30–40/$45–60

➤ The Wonderbra was designed by a Canadian in the 1950s, but did not become really popular until relaunched in the 1990s, featured on roadside posters of model Eva Herzigova under the caption "Hello Boys". The thong was the late 20th century's answer to the "visible panty line", in which the outline of ordinary briefs is clearly visible in figure-hugging trousers. Thongs were a popular alternative, but French knickers were far more comfortable.

Thong   **£5–10/$8–12**   *Wonderbra*   **£20–30/$30–45**

◄ Another example of Marks & Spencer's attempts to regain dominance of the market for women's lingerie, with the help of Agent Provocateur. Sets like these were popular in the 1990s, and women would own several in a variety of colours. Unlike the Wonderbra above, the push-up bra here has no padding. Some fashion writers criticized Marks & Spencer's new fixation with glamour, arguing that plain and practical underwear was on the way back. Others felt "M & S" had lost its edge in the 1980s, when it seemed more interested in selling pre-packed meals.

£20–30/$30–40   *Lingerie set*

➤ In the early 1990s, Calvin Klein had international success with his unisex underwear, especially after it appeared in distinctive black and white advertisements worn by supermodel Kate Moss and pop star Marky Mark. This balcony bra takes advantage of the new stretchy materials to enhance the bust, but it was Klein's product placement that ensured that the brand was the name to display on your underwear in the 1990s.

£20–30/$30–40   *Balcony bra*

Accessories

In the 1990s the "Name Game" thrived as couture houses subsidized their more radical haute couture with the sales of more conventional items bearing the company logo in the High Street. So extreme had the styles on the catwalks become that the *Guardian* newspaper even featured a photograph of a male model in an orange angora sweater with excessively long sleeves, above the headline "Who Wears This Stuff?". Accessories developed their own names and labels with cachet. Just as the Hermès scarf and the Moschino belt were essential in the 1980s, so the 1990s featured such diverse creations as Patrick Cox's Wannabee loafers, crocheted tights by Wolford, Lulu Guinness's handbags, and Phillip Treacy's hats. As before, anything pop icons wore was instantly copied by fans. The Spice Girls were a major influence, helping to popularize a new trend among young women for tattoos (thighs, shoulders, and ankles were favourite areas) and body piercing – a navel ring was a perfect complement to the cropped top. Although the craze was over by the end of the decade, many were left with a permanent reminder of 1990s style.

⬆ The influence of Japanese designers on Western styling had been a major force since the 1970s, but now the fascination with Japanese items took in the "Hello Kitty" range. The childlike cat design appeared on everything, from knapsacks to these wooden-soled, Japanese-style shoes. The affordable, avant-garde equivalent of owning a Gucci handbag, anything with "Hello Kitty" is worth collecting.

"Hello Kitty" shoes   **£40–50/$60–80**

⬇ This shoulder-bag, with the label "Morgan", sums up life in the 1990s. With its shiny, ribbed, synthetic material, the Velcro fastening, the pockets for cards (telephone, credit, and cashpoint), and the holder for the mobile telephone, all the new-found essentials for life could be stored, and even displayed for the approbation of fellow travellers.

£8–10/$12–15   *Bag*

➤ Pashminas (woollen stoles, preferably in cashmere) are a clearly identifiable trend of the late 1990s. Demand threatened to cause shortages of cashmere, but alternatives were just as warm. This one in wool is by Tie Rack, and sold well throughout 1999 in a variety of colours. Despite *Vogue*'s claim in late 1999 that "pashminas are past their sell-by-date", they were advertised in the same issue in Indian cashmere from £450 ($675).

Wool pashmina   **£10–15/$15–25**

◄ This magnificent pair of crocodile boots by Gucci has a metallic finish and thin, tiny heels – the latter were a distinctive design of the time, among the many high, stiletto heels which were prevalent. Boots also enjoyed a resurgence during the 1990s, especially in new fabrics which stretched to fit the leg perfectly.

£220–280/$350–450   *Boots*

➤ ◄ In some cases, trainers left their origins in sportswear behind entirely, and positively hindered mobility. Platform trainers, probably at the extremity of this trend, were worn originally by Geri Halliwell when she was "Ginger Spice" in the Spice Girls. The fascination with the patterns of animal fur continued, whether fake, as here, or real. This pair by Buffalo Shoes is sure to be a 1990s classic. The heels of the Vivienne Westwood shoes beside them demonstrate the differences between 1990s platforms and those of earlier decades. Shoes came in such a wide range of styles that it was possible to wear "Doc." Marten's boots or other flat shoes during the day, and then suffer in stilettos when going out.

Trainers   **£100–120/$150–180**   *Shoes*   **£400–600/$600–800**

Menswear

The 1990s saw men become increasingly interested in fashion. A host of male magazines such as *Maxim* and *GQ* featured designer clothing alongside articles about fast cars, and scantily clad starlets. The fashionable suit was well made by Armani, with Hugo Boss, Gucci, and Versace also among the designer labels leading the way in smart menswear. Sports stars joined the league of the super-rich, becoming new icons of designer style, while pop stars popularized a more casual look – combat trousers, trainers, fishing hats – and more glamorous gear was left to the boy bands and the old stagers. At every level of fashion, having the right label became increasingly important – even supermarkets sold Calvin Klein underwear. But demand for well-made clothes also grew. The New York firm of Brooks Brothers, founded in 1818, became very popular with those men for whom fine tailoring was the primary concern.

➤ Polo shirts were simply too comfortable for men to cast them aside when fashion attempted to dictate that they were out of style – in the 1990s the range of colours and fabrics extended to include pale pinks and cashmere. The original polo shirts were designed in 1934 by the French tennis star René Lacoste, whose nickname "The Crocodile" was seized for his famous crocodile logo. This polo shirt is by Gap, the hugely successful "lifestyle" label which follows in the footsteps of Mary Quant's Ginger Group of the 1960s.

Polo shirt   **£10–20/$15–30**

I want out of the fashion victim brigade. I no longer wish to be recognised as a grand image that sprang from someone else's brain…

Malcolm McLaren, 1992, quoted in the
Penguin Book of Fashion Writing (Viking 1999)

◄ Men who wore socks depicting cartoon characters from *The Beano* or ties with Bart Simpson motifs were no longer a minority in the 1990s; boxer shorts in silk or, as here, cotton, were available in all colours and styles. This pair of cotton boxer shorts is by Tommy Hilfiger (b.1952). Hilfiger is another huge 1990s success story from the USA – the most distinctive thing about his clothes is the unavoidable logo, which, for many, sums up the decade.

£5–10/$8–15   *Underpants*

➤ This Donna Karan suit is typical of her style. The American designer started with sportswear, a route taken by many successful American style leaders. Her clothes are designed, like those of Calvin Klein, for the lives of those who buy them, so she favours draping, wrapping the body in cashmere and jersey. Karan emerged as the foremost fashion designer in the USA in the 1990s: her garments have an understated luxury, and a fit that works particularly well in these new lines of menswear.

£300–500/$500–800   *Suit*

➚ Calvin Klein led fashion across gender boundaries, and here is another example of a logo dominating a garment. Most designers lent their names to mass-production items, often worn by people with little interest in the high style of couture. Sweat-shirts like this had been fashionable since the 1970s when fashion-conscious sports stars, often boxers, introduced them to a wider public.

Sweat-shirt   **£5–10/$8–15**

➤ These Levi 501s are conventional enough: the button fly and straight cut of the 1950s were once again in demand. But the kilt, by Lorna Green (b.1962), is a magnificent example of the work of the deconstructionists. With pocket flaps fastened by safety pins, and unfinished, inside-out seams, it is a classic of the style. Deconstructionist clothes are very collectable as they stand apart from, but heavily influence, mainstream trends.

£30–50/$45–75   *Jeans*   **£100-200/$200–300**   *Kilt*

Unisex

By the end of the 1990s the fascination with retrospective dressing had reached the point where all eras and styles could be clearly identified in the clothes that people wore. Clubbing and dance events, as well as themed nights for every decade since the war, abounded: disco exerted a particular fascination, and 1940s dances were revived around the celebrations in 1994 for the 50th anniversary of D-Day. Unisex fashions reached such a level that entire shops and large sections of flea markets gave themselves over completely to second-hand jeans, trainers, and leather jackets. High Street labels such as Gap and Next sold to both sexes and all ages – the former even branched out into babywear, to be followed by such designers as Donna Karan and Ralph Lauren. Men were inclined to wear more heavily patterned, feminine styles once again, and both sexes experimented with fashions revived from the 1960s and 70s.

↑ One of the lasting, and most commonly seen, effects of the New Age movement was the increased interest throughout the youth market in camouflage designs. Originally fashionable in its army surplus form, camouflage was soon adapted in different colours, and used with other patterns and fabrics, in clothes for children and adults. These two T-shirts are good examples in excellent condition.

£10–15/$15–20   *T-shirts each*

← The Gap is an American clothing manufacturer and international retailer which, although established in the late 1960s, became a worldwide phenomenon in the 1990s, epitomizing the trend for casual separates. Its outlets sell garments for everyone from babies to adults. This unisex sweat-shirt in fleecy material is available in sizes to fit small children to large men.

Sweat-shirt   **£10–15/$15–20**

➤ Football became immensely popular in Europe during the 1990s, and football clubs made fortunes from sales of replica kits, the designs of which were changed at least once every season. Football shirts were casual, everyday wear for male and female fans, although it was usually only boys who also wore the shorts. This shirt is worth more to some because the team, Charlton, were in the English Premiership, and it has been signed by the squad.

Charlton shirt   **£20–25/$30–40**

➤ Cycling and its Lycra tops and shorts had definite cachet in the early 1990s. Fashion leaders among tennis players, footballers, and athletes often wore stretchy Lycra shorts under the official, looser styles. This pair is definitely made for cycling: the sections are cut to fit the shape of the rider, and the gusset is lined with thin, soft chamois.

£8–12/$12–18   *Cycling shorts*

➤ Levis at their best – button-fly, straight-leg 501 jeans. The cargo trousers are another progression from army clothing to mainstream fashion. Military-surplus combat trousers had been fashionable for years, but now loose trousers with knee-high pockets became commonplace to the point of cliché, and were soon being worn by people of all ages.

£20–25/$30–40   *Levi 501s*   **£10–15/$15–20**   *Cargo trousers*

Useful Addresses

Where to buy

20th Century Frocks
65 Steep Hill
Lincoln LN1 1YN
phone: 01522 545916

Antique Clothing Company
282 Portobello Road
London W10 6TE
phone: 020 8964 4830

Linda Bee
Grays Antique Market,
1-7 Davies Mews, London,
W1K 2LP
phone: 020 7629 5921
www.graysantiques.com

Candy Says
phone: 01277 212 134
www.candysays.co.uk

Clothes Junkie
www.clothes-junkie.com

The Girl Can't Help It!
www.thegirlcanthelpit.com

Ebay
www.ebay.com

Echoes
650a Halifax Road
Eastwood, Todmorden
Yorkshire OL14 6DW
phone: 01706 817505

Emporium
330 Creek Road
London SE10 9SW
phone: 020 8305 1670

Etsy
www.etsy.com

It's Vintage Darling
www.itsvintagedarling.com

The Loft
35 Monmouth Street
London WC2H 9DD
phone: 020 7240 3807
www.the-loft.co.uk

Joy Meier
phone: 020 7254 4054

Pop Boutique
6 Monmouth Street
London WC2 9HB
phone: 020 7497 5262
Also Manchester, Liverpool
and Leeds
www.pop-boutique.com

Radio Days Vintage
87 Lower Marsh
London SE1 7AB
phone: 020 7928 0800
www.radiodaysvintage.co.uk

Rellik
8 Golbourne Road, London W10 5NW
phone: 020 8962 0089
www.relliklondon.co.uk

Rennies
47 The Old High Street, Folkestone,
Kent CT20 1RN
phone: 01303 242 427
www.rennart.co.uk

Rokit
225 Camden High Street
London NW1 7DU
phone: 020 7267 3046
Also Brick Lane and Covent Garden,
London
www.rokit.co.uk

Vintage Modes
Grays Antique Market, 1-7 Davies
Mews, London, W1K 2LP
phone: 020 7409 0400
www.graysantiques.com

Vintage to Vogue
28 Milsom Street, Bath BA1 1DG
phone: 01225 337 323
www.vintagetovoguebath.co.uk

Wardrobe
51 Upper North Street
Brighton BN1 3FH
phone: 01273 202201

Deborah Woolf Vintage
28 Church Street,
London NW8 8EP
www.deborahwoolf.com

Velvet Atelier
13-25 Church Street, London NW8
8DT
www.velvetatelier.com

Antique & Vintage Dress Gallery
www.antiquedress.com

The Cats Pajamas
2900 Orchard Avenue, Montoursville
PA 17754
phone: 570 322 5580
www.catspajamas.com

Davenport & Co.
146 Bowdoin Street
Springfield
MA 01109
phone: 413 781 1505
www.davenportandco.com

Neet-O-Rama
93 W. Main St., Somerville, NJ 08876,
USA
phone: 001 908 722 4600
www.neetstuff.com

Rusty Zipper Vintage Clothing
phone: 866 387 5944
www.rustyzipper.com

Screaming Mimis
382 Lafayette Street,
New York, NY 10003
phone: 212 677 6464
www.screamingmimis.com

A Victorian Elegance
phone: 813 436 4313
www.victorianelegance.com

Vintage Eyewear Of Nyc Inc.
phone: 001 646 319 9222

The Way We Wore
334 S La Brea Ave
Los Angeles, CA 90036
phone: 323 937 0878
www.thewaywewore.com

Antiques Markets

Alfie's Antique Market
13–25 Church Street
London NW8
Open Tuesday to Saturday
www.alfiesantiques.com

Camden Market
Chalk Farm Road, London NW1
Open daily
www.camdenlock.net

Grays Antique Market
1-7 Davies Mews,
London, W1K 2LP
phone: 020 7409 0400
www.graysantiques.com

Greenwich Market
Greenwich Church Street
London SE10
*Vintage markets Tuesdays, Thursdays
and Fridays*
www.shopgreenwich.co.uk

Portobello Market
Portobello Road
London W11
Open Friday and Saturday
www.portobelloroad.co.uk

Annex Antique Fair & Market
6th Avenue from 24th to 27th St, New
York
phone: 212 243 5343
Open Saturday and Sunday

The Garage
112 West 25th Street, btween 6th and
7th Ave, New York
phone: 212 647 0707
Open Saturday and Sunday

Auction Houses

Christies
85 Old Brompton Road
London SW7 3LD
phone: 020 7930 6074
www.christies.com

Bonhams
Montpelier Street
London SW7 1HH
phone: 020 7393 3900
7601 W. Sunset Boulevard
Los Angeles CA 90046
phone: 323 850 7500
www.bonhams.com

William Doyle Galleries
175 East 87th Street
New York NY 10128
phone: 212 427 2730
www.doylenewyork.com

Leslie Hindman Auctioneers
1338 West Lake Street, Chicago, IL
60607
phone: 312 280 1212
www.lesliehindman.com

Kerry Taylor Auctions Ltd
249-253 Long Lane
London SE1 4PR
phone: 020 8676 4600
www.kerrytaylorauctions.com

Specialist Fairs

Adams Antiques Fairs
phone: 020 7254 4054
www.adamsantiquesfairs.co.uk

Frock Me
Vintage fashion fairs
www.frockmevintagefashion.com

Caring for your collection

Vintage clothes need to be treated with care and attention. For starters, you will need a lot of acid-free tissue paper in which to store garments – any friendly dealer should be happy to supply you with large quantities at reasonable cost.

Dresses, skirts, and blouses should be hung on padded hangers, and protected from dust with cotton or plastic covers, but make sure that air can circulate through these covers. Cupboards and wardrobes should be protected with anti-moth pouches and sprays, as moth damage, like any other damage, seriously affects the value of an item.

Hats should be held gently in shape with a padding of tissue paper. Gloves, underwear, and heavy, delicate items like beaded dresses are best stored flat between layers of tissue paper. Buckles and buttons need special attention. Some are spectacular, and impossible to replace, so make sure that you secure any loose button with cotton thread as soon as you notice it.

Shoes pose one of the major difficulties in collecting and wearing vintage clothes. Old shoes are best stored in racks or in boxes, and, again, gently held in shape with tissue paper. Never wear vintage shoes that have been bought unworn. If you have a used and sturdy pair you want to show off at a special event, wear them indoors only and change into less precious footwear when you leave – never wear vintage shoes in wet weather. There is no way of avoiding some punishment to shoes however careful you are, so it is perhaps better to look for modern styles and shapes which mimic those of the period you collect, and use these instead – you can do this with hosiery too.

If you want to wear your vintage clothes, you will need to have to have them cleaned properly. Sturdy items can be dry cleaned, so try and establish a good relationship with your local dry cleaners. Some may find the prospect of handling vintage clothes a chore, but others will enjoy cleaning something a little different and treat your collection with special care – they may even give you discount for bulk orders. Plastic, metal and glass buttons, buckles, or other decorations should all be removed or covered with tissue and tin foil before cleaning, or they will smash.

Clothes from the earlier part of the century, designer labels, beaded dresses, and feathered or delicate fabrics will all need very specialist cleaning and care. Talk to the textiles experts at your local museum or university, who are usually very helpful – the Victoria & Albert Museum in London, for instance, holds a list of freelance conservators who restore items to museum standard. Don't forget that specialist dealers are often immensely knowledgeable, and that your first source of useful information should be the person selling the garment to you!

Select Bibliography

Bond, David, *The Guinness Guide to Twentieth Century Fashion*, Guinness Superlatives Ltd., 1981.

Caldwell, Doreen, *And All was Revealed – Ladies Underwear 1907–1980*, Arthur Barker, 1981.

Chenoune, Farid, *A History of Men's Fashion*, Flammarion, 1993.

Clancy, Deirdre, *Costume Since 1945*, Herbert Press, 1996.

Hall, Caroline, *The Thirties in Vogue*, Octopus Books, 1984.

Hawthorne, Rosemary, *Bras*, Souvenir Press, 1992.

Hawthorne, Rosemary, *Knickers*, Souvenir Press, 1991.

Hawthorne, Rosemary, *Stockings and Suspenders*, Souvenir Press, 1993.

Jenkins, Alan, *The Twenties*, Book Club Associates, 1974.

Mitchell, Graham, *The Roaring Twenties*, Batsford, 1986.

Mulvagh, Jane, *Vogue History of Twentieth Century Fashion*, Viking, 1988.

O'Hara Callan, Georgina, *Dictionary of Fashion and Fashion Designers*, Thames & Hudson, 1998.

Owen, Elizabeth, *Fashion in Photographs 1920–1940*, Batsford, 1993.

Robinson, Julian, *Fashion in the 30s*, Oresko Books, 1978.

Stevenson, Pauline, *Edwardian Fashion*, Ian Allen, 1980.

Tierney, Tom, *Schiaparelli Fashion Review*, Dover Publications, 1988.

The Long Weekend – A Social History of Great Britain 1919–1939, Hutchinson, 1940; repr. 1985.

Also available, and very helpful to the collector, are magazines, too numerous to mention individually, devoted both to 20th-century fashion and to each of the periods covered in this book.

Glossary

A

acetate A man-made fabric created in Germany in the 19th century. Commercially produced by the company British Celanese in 1920, the fabric has been in use ever since.

acrylic Synthetic yarn often used as a cheaper, lightweight wool substitute. Trade name Acrilan refers to acrylic.

A-line A popular dress shape from the mid-1950s, the skirt flares giving a shape like two sides of a triangle from the bust or waist, with the hem of the garment making the third side.

appliqué A shape in contrasting fabric sewn on to a garment.

artificial silk Invented in the late 19th century, named Rayon after a competition to find a new name in 1924, it is made from cellulose. Artificial silk hangs like silk and dyes easily. First used commercially for stockings before World War I, it became immensely popular in the 1920s for all sorts of garments. Viscose rayon became the most common form after World War II.

B

Ballets Russes Ballet company lead by Serge Diaghilev and featuring the work of designers such as Leon Bakst which had an enormous influence with its rich colours and fabrics, inspired by Russian and Oriental styling. The company's first European tour took place to great acclaim in 1909.

basque Also known as a peplum, a very short skirt-shape sewn onto a bodice or jacket.

batwing sleeve Very popular during the 1930s, this is a sleeve with no shoulder for the armhole, being instead an extension of the waist. Also known as a dolman.

bell bottoms Trousers worn by men and women, originally worn by sailors, they were cut from knee to ankle in the shape of a bell. Versions known as hipsters were popular from the 1960s.

boiler suit An all-in-one garment with long sleeves and a zipped or buttoned front. Originally worn by manual workers, the boiler suit became essential wear for women at work in World War II, especially in a version known as the "siren suit".

"bomber" jacket A loose-cut jacket elasticated at the waist and first worn by American bomber pilots, it became popular with both sexes. Variations were known as "varsity", "battle", and "Eisenhower" jackets.

bouclé A crinkled, looped yarn, from the French term for curled.

brassière A 20th-century fashion, invented in the early 1900s and patented in 1914, the brassière became known as the bra by the end of the 1920s, when versions with adjustable straps and elastic became popular.

brocade Rich fabric with a raised design woven into it.

bustier An item of underwear since the 19th century, it combined the functions of the brassière and camisole and became popular during the late 20th century for use as outerwear.

C

calico Heavy-duty cotton-based fabric, it was used for most underwear until the early part of the 19th century.

cambric Cotton fabric of French origin finished with a gloss on one side, it was very popular in the 19th century.

camiknickers Combination of camisoles and knickers, usually fastened with small buttons between the legs, which took various forms during the 20th century.

camisole Originally worn over the corset to protect the dress. Late 20th-century versions are often in silk, satin, and synthetic or fine cotton materials.

catsuit An all-in-one garment for women fashionable in the 1960s and 70s.

chemise A loose, simple garment, the chemise is the layer of underwear closest to the body, worn under the corset in the 19th and early 20th centuries.

chesterfield Named after the fourth Earl of Chesterfield in the 1830s, a type of man's overcoat with a fitted waist and velvet collar which has remained popular, with minor variations, ever since as a style for men.

chiffon Lightweight sheer fabric.

ciré Method which adds a wax finish to make a shiny waterproof fabric.

corset Originally a stiffened version of the bodice, the corset is the garment which shapes and squeezes the torso into a particular silhouette. Whalebone and lacing shapings were replaced by plastic and elastic early in the 20th century, but by the end of the century, leather and metallic versions were worn as outerwear, and featured foam and Lycra.

court shoes Women's footwear with pointed toes and low to medium heels. Known as the pump in the USA.

crêpe Crinkled texture given to a fabric.

Cuban heels Short, straight, thick heels originally worn on the boots of South American gauchos.

D
Dacron Trade name of a polyester-based fabric manufactured by DuPont in the 1950s.

décolleté Low neckline on a dress or a blouse, particularly fashionable on evening dresses of the late 19th and the early 20th centuries, and on garments of the 1950s.

deconstructionists Influential group of late 20th-century designers who broke fashion down to its essentials and rebuilt the structure of garments, emphasizing such features as raw, inside-out seams, and used experimental techniques in dyeing.

denim Originally *serge de Nîmes*, from the French town of that name, a cotton twill fabric used for workwear until the 1960s, when it became immensely popular as street fashion.

Doctor Marten's Boots Invented in Germany but developed in Britain. Originally workwear, they were fashionable from the 1960s with "skinheads", and with everyone else from the 1980s.

E
empire line A high-waisted, low-cut style of dress first made popular by the Empress Josephine, wife of Napoleon, in the early 19th century, and revived in the early 20th century by Paul Poiret.

epaulette Originally a strap on a military jacket, it now refers to any shoulder decoration.

ethnic Styles of clothing inspired by garments which originate with peasant communities, and generally those styles borrowed from outside Western Europe and the USA.

F
façonné Textiles in which motifs or patterns are woven into the fabric.

faggoting Embroidery in which the threads are gathered together to join or decorate fabric in the style of a bundle of sticks, or faggot.

frock coat Originally a military-style coat which became formal dress for men in the 19th century, and which was replaced by the suit in the 20th century.

furbelow Originally a fur trimming, it was attached to the hem of a long skirt to protect it against dirt and damage.

G
gamine A look made popular in the 1950s by film actress Audrey Hepburn. Her short, cropped hair, slim figure, and boyish, elfin face contrasted with the full-figured, blousey style of the time.

grunge Originally a musical movement in the late 1980s and early 1990s, grunge rejected fashion, especially expensive clothing and close-fitting garments. A successor to the 1960s hippy movement, with its anti-consumerist, anti-materialist philosophy, it inspired as many designers as punk had done in the 1970s.

H
Harris tweed A coarse, woollen fabric originating from islands in the Outer Hebrides, off the coast of Scotland. Intermittently fashionable since it was first imported in the 19th century, tweed has a distinctive aroma when wet.

Hawaiian shirt Made popular by American tourists in Hawaii in the 1950s, a loose-fitting, brightly coloured, short-sleeved shirt, usually patterned with motifs reminiscent of tropical islands.

hippy The term given to followers of the anti-materialistic 1960s movement which had an enormous influence on fashion. Exotic fabrics, second-hand clothes, long hair and long hemlines, psychedelic patterns, and unisex fashions all had their origins in the hippy movement.

"hobble" skirt Introduced by Paul Poiret in the early 1900s, "hobble" skirts were narrow cut, and severely restricted the stride of the wearer so she could take only small steps – hence the name. They became fashionable from about 1910 and were complemented with a tunic, especially in the lampshade style.

hourglass shape Popular during the late 19th century and the Edwardian era of the early 20th century, the hourglass shape used padding and corsetry to emphasize the bust and hips.

J

jacquard A decorative style in woven fabric – its eponymous inventor devised a system of punched cards to direct the pattern of different coloured threads in the weaving process.

jersey Stretchy, knitted fabric originating from the Channel Island of Jersey in the late 19th century. Popular during the 1920s and 30s with designers wanting free-flowing lines to their garments.

K

kaftan A loose, full-length garment often highly decorated, and very popular during the 1970s.

kick pleat Inverted pleat near the hemline giving increased freedom of movement, especially on tight skirts.

L

lamé Fabric into which metallic threads are woven, popular for eveningwear.

lisle The name given to a cotton yarn used for stockings, originating from the French town of Lille.

Lurex Brand name for a yarn with metallic fibres, introduced in the USA in the 1940s.

Lycra Brand name of a synthetic fabric introduced by DuPont in the 1950s, Lycra is known for its elasticity. After initially gaining popularity in sportswear and in hosiery, Lycra became widely used in the 1980s in garments of all kinds.

M

maxi Name given to floor-length clothes, especially maxi-coats and maxi-skirts, in the late 1960s and early 1970s.

midi Name given to the calf-length clothes of the early 1970s, less popular than the maxi and mini lengths.

mod Follower of a 1960s urban teenage movement whose followers rode motor scooters, wore sharp, Italian-style suits and parkas, and had short styled hair.

moiré Process which gives a water-stained effect, often used on silk.

mourning clothes Disproportionate quantities of black mourning wear from the Victorian and Edwardian eras survive today, and it is popular with collectors.

N

New Look The name given to Dior's Corolle line. The full skirts, fitted bodices, and small waists required yards of material and stiffening when post-war shortages were at their most severe.

Norfolk jacket Initially worn by gentlemen on country pursuits in the late 19th century, this was a belted wool jacket with patch pockets and box pleats.

Nylon Synthetic fibre invented by groups of American and British chemists. First used for hosiery in the United States in 1939, nylon stockings were virtually unobtainable in Europe until the 1950s. An immensely versatile fibre, it was used on a wide range of garments in the 1950s and 60s.

O

Organdie A fine, translucent cotton muslin which is usually stiffened.

"Oxford bags" Straight-legged, wide trousers worn with turn-ups by fashionable male undergraduates at Oxford during the 1920s, they were popular again, as a unisex item, in the 1970s.

P

panne Type of velvet in which the pile is crushed in one direction, giving a shimmering effect.

patent Finish which gives a high gloss effect to leather, used especially on handbags, boots, and shoes since the 1930s. Very fashionable in the 1960s.

petticoat Originally the name given to a man's undershirt, the petticoat had been an essential item of underwear for hundreds of years until the 20th century when it metamorphosed into the slip. Traditional, flouncy cotton petticoats enjoyed a brief revival during the 1970s.

platform shoes Thick soles to shoes that were introduced by Ferragamo in 1938, platforms were popular during the 1940s, 70s, and 90s.

polyester Introduced in the 1940s, it was first used in home furnishings. Polyester has been widely used in clothing of all types and styles since the 1950s.

R

Raglan A sleeve seam which runs diagonally from the armpit to the neck, especially one which obviates the need for a shoulder seam.

Rayon See artificial silk

ready-to-wear Designer collections which are mass produced and can be bought off the peg.

roll-on An elasticated girdle which replaced the corset after World War II.

S

safari suits Made fashionable during the 1960s by Ted Lapidus and Yves Saint Laurent, based on the style of clothing worn by European men on safari. The jacket was belted and had patch pockets.

serge Twill-weave, worsted fabric originally used for working clothes and military uniforms, wool-based serge became the basic fabric for men's suits.

sheath Dress with figure-hugging skirt and shaped bodice, popular in the 1950s.

shirtwaister Style of dress based on the design of a man's shirt, made popular in the 1940s, and later in the 1970s by the designer, Diane von Furstenberg.

sportswear Term used in the USA for daywear.

street style Styles worn by teenagers and others, often with little money or interest in conventional clothing, for whom clothes make a political or social comment, rather than a fashion statement. An increasingly influential source of inspiration for fashion designers in the 20th century, overtly so since the 1960s.

T

taffeta Thin, stiffened fabric, often with a glossy finish, used for eveningwear until 1900, and often for petticoats thereafter.

tea gown One of the many dresses into which the Edwardian lady would change during the day, the tea gown was worn indoors and allowed the wearer to loosen her tight corsets.

tracksuit Suit worn by athletes comprising loose, sweat-shirt-style top and loose trousers, elasticated at the waist and ankles. Tracksuits became part of mainstream fashion during the 1970s fitness boom, and were soon adapted as practical, easy-care garments by people of all ages and shapes. Velour versions were particularly popular in the 1970s.

twinset Knitted set of cardigan and sweater, the latter usually short-sleeved. Introduced during the 1930s.

U

unisex Clothing which can be worn by either or both sexes, typically T-shirts, jeans, footwear, and caps, using exotic or colourful patterns. Unisex clothing arrived in the 1960s and, since then, has consistently remained part of mainstream fashion.

Utility wear A scheme introduced in 1941 in response to shortages in wartime Britain, it prohibited unnecessary elements in design. Some of the best-known British designers took part, so garments were often imaginatively made, and prices were controlled. The scheme continued until 1951. Utility clothing is popular with collectors today because of its distinctive styling.

V

Vogue Magazine started in the USA in 1892, *Vogue* is now the bible of high style in fashion and the arts, with editions throughout the world.

W

wet look Alternative name for ciré.

worsted Hardwearing fabric made from wool.

Z

zip Originally introduced in the USA in 1893, the zip, or zipper, was first used on belts issued to soldiers during World War I. By the 1930s it had started to appear regularly on women's clothing, and it had become commonplace by the end of World War II.

Index

Page numbers in *italic* refer to illustrations, those in **bold** refer to main entries

A

A-line 13, 74
accessories
  belts 27, 55, 74, 75, *110, 126*
  fans 27
  feather boas 27
  glasses 82, 97
  jewellery 22, 37, *64*, 110
  parasols *26*, 54
  scarves 33, *40, 54*
  stoles 26, 54, 55, 82, *143*
  watches 97
  see also bags; boots; hats;
  shoes
acetate *119*, 152
acrylic 77
Adidas *127*
Aesthetic movement 10
Agnès B *136*
American design 11, 13, 15,
  68, 78, 102
appliqué *47, 77*, 152
Armani, Giorgio *129*
army surplus 15, 104, *146*, 147
Art Deco 31, 89
Art Nouveau 10, 17, 24
art silk 10, 32, *34*, 52, *66*, 152
Ashley, Laura 101, 102, *103*
Astaire, Fred 56

B

bags
  clutch 37, *40, 41, 54,*
  110, 126
  evening *23*, 27, *41, 65*
  handbags 68, 82, 83, 96
  shoulder *83, 96, 110, 126, 142*
Bakelite 47, 48, 54
Bakst, Leon 10, 33, 152
Balenciaga, Cristobal 59, 73, 88
Ballet Russes 10, 18, 33, 152

Balmain, Pierre 74, 75
Banlon 123
Bates, John 91
beadwork 22, *23*, 36, *78, 79*
Beatles, The 13, 99
Beene, Geoffrey 105
belts 27, *55*, 74, 75, *110, 126*
Benetton *139*
berets 69, 82, 97, *111*
Best, George 98
bias-cutting 11, *51*
Biba 98, 102, *107*
"Big Look" 14, 110
Blass, Bill 122
blouses 32, 33, 48, *61*, 74, 90,
  102–3, 106
Body Map 118
body shape 10, 24, 38, 48, 52,
  66, 80
body stockings 94
boilersuit 60, 152
boleros 37
boots 26, 70, 96, 97, 98, *111,*
  127, 143
Bow, Clara 11
bra slips 95
bracelets 37
braces 70
Brando, Marlon 84
bras
  bustiers 95, *125*
  Eighties *125*
  Fifties *80*
  Forties *66*
  history 11, 38, 152
  inflatable 80
  Nineties *140, 141*
  "no-bra" 94
  padded 80, *95, 141*
  push-up *141*
  seam-free *109*

Seventies *108, 109*
Sixties 94, *95*
  slips 95
sports *140*
strapless *66, 109*
Thirties *52*
Twenties *38*
underwired 95, *141*
Wonderbra 140, *141*
British design 13, 15, 29, 32,
  84, 87, 118
brooches *64*
Bruce, Lisa 120
bustiers 95, *125*
buttons 34, 47, 48, *61, 62, 75*

C

camiknickers 38, *53*, 152
camisoles *24, 124*, 152
canes 29
caps 13, *28*, 29, *36*, 97
cardigans 32, *49*, 76, 77, *78*, 155
Cardin, Pierre 98, 99
Cassini, Oleg 87
catsuits *107*, 152
celluloid 27, 41
Chanel, Coco 10, 11, 32, 46, 78
cinema, influence of 11, 27,
  46, 73, 74, 84
ciré 96, 153, 155
Clark, Ossie *106*
Classical movement 10, 18
cleaning 19, 33, 92, 106, 113,
  150
Clements Ribiero *138*
cloaks *42*
coats
  Afghan *114*
  "Crombie" 84
  and dress sets *47, 48*
  duffel 70

Edwardian *18*
  evening *36, 37*
  Fifties 84
  Forties *62*
  frock 28, 153
  greatcoats 62
  leather *43*
  motoring *18, 43*
  New Look 62
  overcoats 28, 152
  PVC 89, *91*
  rain 89, *91*
  Sixties 89, *91*
  swagger *63*
  Twenties 34, *42, 43*
  uniform 62
Colbert, Claudette, 46
collars 29, 32, 42, 70, *74*, 103,
  115, 121
Collins, Joan 122
colour 20, 23, 33, 38, 48, 49,
  51, 108
Comme des Garçons 137
"Corform" 96
corsets 10, 17, 18, *25*, 39, 52,
  117, 153
cosmetics 11, 27, 40, 54, 97, 112
cotton 43, 108
Courrèges, André 13, 88, 91, 97
Courtaulds 107
cravats 29
Crawford, Joan 46, 55
crimplene 105
crochet *102, 110, 111*
culottes 105, *120*
cycling shorts *147*

D

Damart 125
dance, influence of 10, 14, 18,
  22, 23, 36, 39, 92

Dean, James 84
deconstructionism 145, 153
Delaunay, Sonia 33
denim 101, 111, *113, 115*, 153
Depression 11, 45, 49
designer labels 15, 32, 95, 126, 142
detachable trimmings 19, 22
devoré *36, 50*
Diaghilev, Serge 10, 33, 152
Diana, Princess of Wales 15, 117, 133
Dicel 107
Diesel *134*
Dietrich, Marlene 46
Dior, Christian 12, 59, 60, 62, 74, 92, 124, 154
Dolce & Gabbana *136*
dresses
    appliquéd *47*
    beaded *22, 36, 79*
    bias-cut *51*
    décolleté *22, 23*
    Edwardian 10, 17, *18–23*
    Eighties *118, 119, 120, 123*
    Fifties *74–5, 78–9*
    Forties *60, 64–5*
    Jean Muir *119*
    knitted *92*
    military look *104, 118*
    mini *88–9, 93, 122*
    Nineties *136, 137, 138, 139*
    "prom" *79*
    ruched *65*
    Seventies *104, 106–7*
    sheath *74, 78*, 117, 155
    shift *88, 92*
    shirtwaister *60*, 155
    Sixties *88–9, 92–3*
    Thirties *47–8, 50–1*
    tunic *19*
    Twenties *33–5, 37*
    Utility *60*
    see also kaftans
dry cleaning 92, 113, 150

E
Edward, Prince of Wales 11, 42, 43
Edward VII, King of England 28
Edwardian fashions 10, **16–29**, 84, 85
Egyptian influence 11, 40, 41
Eighties fashions 15, **116–31**
elastic 11, 24, 38, 52
ethnic look 14, 96, *104, 106, 110, 114*, 153

F
Fairbanks, Douglas 11, 42
fans *27*
feather boas *27*
Ferragamo, Salvatore 68, 83, 154
Fifties fashions 13, **72–85**
fishtails 10, *139*
fitness movement, influence of 12, 45, 102, 109, 120, 124, 140
flappers 31, 36
football shirts 15, *147*
Forties fashions 12, **58–71**
Fortuny, Mariano 10, 17
foundation garments 52, 80, *94*
fur 13, *34,* 54, *76, 135*

G
Gable, Clark 56
"Gaiety Girls" 23
Galliano, John 15, 92, *121, 122*, 133
Gap *144, 146*
Garbo, Greta 12, 31, 54
garters 25, *38*
Gaultier, Jean-Paul 102, 117
Gernreich, Rudi 94
Gibson Girls 17
girdles 80, *94*
Givenchy, Hubert 73
"Glam Rock" 14, 111, 114
glasses *82, 97*

gloves 21, *55*, 65
Gossard 80
Goth style 124, 126
Grunge style 133, 153
Gucci *143*

H
H-line 13
hairstyles 15, 60, 82, 87, 90, 92, 112, 126
Hamnett, Katherine 130
handkerchiefs *54*
Harlow, Jean 46, 52
Hartnell, Norman 32
hats
    boater 29, 42
    bowler 29
    cartwheel 10, *21*
    cloche 40, *41*
    "coolie" 82
    cossack 82
    crochet *110, 111*
    Edwardian 20, *21, 28, 29*
    Eighties *119*
    evening *50*
    Fifties *82*
    Forties *69*
    Homburg 28, 29, *56*
    military look *69*
    panama *42*
    pillbox *87*
    Seventies *110*
    "Shoe" *55*
    Sixties *97*
    "slouch" *54*
    smoking *28*
    Thirties *50,* 54, 55
    top *29*
    Twenties 36, 40, *41, 42*
    see also berets; caps
"Hello Kitty" range *142*
Hepburn, Audrey 73, 153
Hepburn, Katherine 12, 46
Hilfiger, Tommy *144*
hippy look 14, 87, 96, 98, 101,

112, *114*, 153
Holah, David 118
home dressmaking 35, 53, 61
hot pants 14, 101
hourglass shape 10, 17, 18, 154
Hulanicki, Barbara *see* Biba

I
Italian design 13, 73, 74, 82, 84, *126*

J
jackets
    bed *67*
    "bomber" 13, *84, 112*, 152
    casual *56, 128*
    dinner 28, 56
    drape *84*
    Edwardian *21*
    Eighties *118, 119, 121, 122, 128*
    evening *36, 50, 51, 64*, 122
    Fifties *76, 84*
    Forties *63, 64*
    Galliano *121*
    knitted *103*
    leather *130*
    Nineties *134, 135*
    Norfolk 154
    Seventies *103, 105, 112, 113, 115*
    Sixties *90*
    smoking 28
    Thirties *50, 51, 56*
    Twenties *34, 36, 37*
    varsity 13, *84, 112*, 152
    women's *34, 105*
Jagger, Mick 114
James, Charles 65, 78
Japanese design 14, 101, 110, 117, *123, 137, 142*
jeans 84, 98, 114, *115, 145, 147*
jerkins *113*
jersey 32, 107, 154
jewellery 22, 37, *64*, 110
jumpers *61, 77, 78, 135*

K

kaftans *104*, 114, 154
Karan, Donna 134, 138, *145*,
    146
Kawakubo, Rei *137*
Kayser 52, 53
Kelly, Grace 74
Kennedy, Jackie 87
Kenzo 14, 101
kick pleats *47, 49, 77*, 154
kilts *145*
Klein, Calvin 15, 102, *141*,
    144, *145*
Klimt, Gustav 10
knickers *24, 37, 39, 53, 66,
    108, 125, 141*
knitting
    hand 61, 103
    machine 10, 32, 77

L

labels 53, 77, 123
Lacoste, René 144
Lagerfeld, Karl 122
Lanvin, Jeanne 10, 17
Lapidus, Ted 99
Lauren, Ralph 15, 102, 146
leather 96, 130, 136
leg warmers 109
leggings *120, 121, 137*
leotards 109, *120*
lifestyle influences 17, 22, 54,
    60, 78, 87, 122, 140
lingerie *see* underwear
logos 15, *96, 111,* 113, 131,
    144, 145
loons *115*
Lycra 136

M

Mackintosh, Charles Rennie 18
Madonna 117, 124, 136
Maidenform 95
make-up *see* cosmetics
Marks & Spencer *61,* 108, *140,
    141*

McCardell, Clare 13, 77
McQueen, Alexander 15, *135*
merchandising 15, *96, 111,*
    113, *131, 144, 145*
Miyake, Issey *123*
Monroe, Marilyn 73, 80
Morton, Digby 60
Moschino, Franco *137*
Moygashel 60
Mugler, Thierry 102, *123*
Muir, Jean *119*
mules *78, 83*

N

negligées 81
Negri, Pola 36
net *79, 81*
New Look 12, 59, 60, *62,* 154
New Romantics 117, 126,
    127
nightdresses *81, 94, 140*
Nike 127, *131*
Nineties fashions 15, **132–47**
Nordheim, Thomas von *135*
nylon 12, 66, *80,* 108, 154

O

Op Art 89, 91

P

padded shoulders 15, 118,
    119, 122
Palmers 53
pants *see* trousers
parasols *26,* 54
pashminas *143*
patchwork 110, *115*
Patou, Jean 11, 32, 46
Perspex 96
petticoats *25,* 53, 80, *81, 95,*
    154
plastic 11, 27, 41, 47, 48, 54
Playtex 94
pleats *47, 49, 77, 107*
Poiret, Paul 10, 17, 22, 24, 38
polyester 102, 105

Pop Art *96, 97,* 113
pop music, influence of 73, 84,
    87, 111, 112, 130, 133, 142
Prada, Miuccia 133, *138*
Pre-Raphaelites 18
psychedelic patterns *88, 96*
pullovers *71, 115*
Puma *127*
punk style 15, 101, 102, 112,
    117, *130*
PVC *89, 91, 128*
pyjamas 53
pyjamas, lounging *46*

Q

Quant, Mary 13, 87, 95

R

Rabanne, Paco 13, 88
Reagan, Nancy 117
Red or Dead *139*
Reebok 127
Reger, Janet 125
Renta, Oscar de la 122
retro style 84, 85, 98, 103, 111,
    136, 146
Rigg, Diana 91
Riley, Bridget 91
Roberts, Patricia 103
roll-ons 66, 94, 108, 155
Romanticism 10–11, 12, 45,
    46, 50
rubber 52, *131*
ruching 65, *125*
Russell, Jane 80

S

"S" shape 10, 17, 18
"sac" dress 13, 74
Sacha 111
Saint Laurent, Yves 87, 88, 97,
    99, 112
Sassoon, Vidal 13, 90
scarves 33, *40,* 54
Schiaparelli, Elsa 46, 55, 67
separates 20, 32

Seventies fashions 14–15,
    101–15
shirts
    bowling 84
    casual 13, *85,* 99
    Edwardian 28
    Eighties 128
    Fifties 84, 85
    football *147*
    Forties *71*
    Nineties *144*
    polo *144*
    Seventies *112, 113, 114*
    Sixties 99
    striped 28, *71*
    Twenties 42
    see also T-shirts
shoes
    Edwardian *26, 29*
    Eighties *127*
    espadrilles *111*
    evening *51, 78*
    Fifties *78, 83,* 84
    Forties *68, 69, 70*
    loafers 68
    Nineties 133, *142, 143*
    peep-toe *40*
    platform *111, 143,* 154
    sandals *111*
    Seventies *100,* 110, *111*
    Sixties *89, 96*
    sling-backs 89
    slip-ons 68
    spats 28, *29*
    stilettos 13, *83*
    strapless 83
    Thirties *51*
    Twenties *40*
    Utility *68, 69*
    wedge 68
    "winkle-pickers" *83,* 84
    see also mules; slippers;
        trainers
shorts 15, *120, 147*
Shrimpton, Jean 88, 94
silk 12, 33, 124

silk, artificial 10, 32, *34*, 52, *66*, 152
Sixties fashions 13–14, **86–99**
ski-wear *131*
skinny ribs *103*
skirts
  crinoline 79, 118
  Fifties *77*
  Forties *71*
  hemlines 11, 13, 14, 17, 21, 22, 23, 36
  "hobble" 10, 17, 18, 38, 153
  maxi 14, 101, 106, *107*
  midi 14, *91*, 101, 106
  mini 13, 14, 88, 91, 133, *136*
  Nineties 133, *136*
  puffball 118
  ra-ra 118
  Seventies 101, *104*
  Sixties 88, *91*
  Thirties *48*
sleeves *19*, 48, *50*, 61, *65*, *102*, 105, 128, 152
slippers *78*, *83*
slips *see* bra slips; petticoats
socks *109*
Space Age look 13, 88, 91, 97, 99
Spice Girls 133, 142, 143
sports, influence of 10, 11, 32
sportswear 77, *109*, *120*, 130, *131*, *140*, *146*, *147*, 155
Stephen, John 98
Stewart, Stevie 118
Stiebel, Victor 75
stockings
  decorated *25*, *39*, *80*, *124*
  nylon 12, 66, *67*, *80*, 140
  patterned 95
  seamed 124
  silk *39*, 52
stoles 26, 54, 55, 82, *143*
street style 88, 102, 112, 155
suits
  Armani *129*
  Cardin 13, *99*

Chanel 32, *49*
double-breasted *57*, 70, *71*
Edwardian *21*, 28, *29*
Eighties 117, 118, *119*, 128, *129*
Fifties 76, 84
Forties 60, *61*, *63*, 70, *71*
Nineties 135, 144, *145*
power 15, 117, 118
Seventies *105*, *113*
shell 130
siren 60
Sixties 99
Thirties *49*, 57
three-piece 10, 28
trouser *105*
tweed 57
Twenties 32
Utility *71*
zoot 13, 70
suspenders 25, 52, *67*, 80, 140, *141*
sweat-shirts *145*
sweaters *see* jumpers
synthetics 77, 90, 102, 104, 105, 107, 119, 123
  see also nylon

T
T-shirts 15, 108, *130*, *131*, *137*, *146*
taffeta 24, 75, 79, 155
tank tops *115*
teddies *125*
"Teddy Boys" 84
teenagers, influence of 13, 83
television, influence of 15, 122
Terylene 90
Thaarup, Aage 68
Thatcher, Margaret 15, 102, 117, 118
Thirties fashions 11–12, **44–57**
thongs *141*
ties *70*, 85, 113
tights 94, 95, *124*

tops 14, *23*, *115*, *120*, *134*, *139*
  short *74*
tracksuits *131*, 155
trainers *127*, *143*
trains 10, 22, 23, *64*, *139*
Tricel 107
trousers
  bell bottoms 152
  cargo *147*
  Chinos 128
  combat *147*
  corduroy 56, 57
  evening 64, 78, 106
  flannel 43, *57*
  flared 101, *113*, *115*
  gaucho 13
  "Oxford bags" 42, 154
  "pedal pushers" *74*
  peg-top *29*
  "pirate pants" *74*
  plus fours *43*, 57
  PVC *128*
  slacks 98
  suits *105*
  wide 13, 42, *43*, *136*
  women's 12, *46*, 60, *74*
  see also jeans; shorts
tunics 10, *19*, 22, 153
tuxedos 56
Twenties fashions 11, **30–43**
Twiggy 13, 89

U
underwear
  boxer shorts *144*
  bra slips 95
  camiknickers 38, 53, 152
  camisoles *24*, *124*, 152
  corsets 10, 17, 18, *25*, *39*, 52, 117, 153
  foundation garments 52, 80, *94*
  garters *25*, *38*
  girdles 80, 94
  knickers *24*, *37*, *39*, *53*, *66*, *108*, *125*, *141*

men's 56, *144*
petticoats *25*, *53*, 80, *81*, *95*, 154
roll-ons 66, 94, 108, 155
suspenders 25, 52, *67*, 80, 140, *141*
thermal *125*
thongs *141*
vests 56, *125*
"waspies" 80
  see also bras; nightdresses; stockings; tights
Ungaro 122
Union Jack motif *96*
unisex 14–15, 104, **114–15**, **130–1**, **146–7**
Utility clothes 12, 59, *60*, *61*, *63*, *67*, *68*, *69*, 155

V
Valentino, Rudolph 11, 31, 42
velvet *36*, *50*
Versace, Gianni 133, *137*
vests 56, *125*
viscose 104, 107, 152
Voyage *134*

W
waistcoats 28, 85, 98, *102*, *114*, *129*
waistlines 11, *19*, *20*, 24, 33, 51, 74
wartime clothes 11, 12, 17, 22, 23, 59
"waspies" 80
watches 97
Westwood, Vivienne 15, 101, 102, *127*, 133, *135*, *143*
Wolsey 94
Wonderbras 140, *141*

Y
Yamamoto, Kansai 14, 101

Z
zips 46, *103*

Acknowledgments

The publisher and author would like to thank the following people for supplying pictures for use in the book or for allowing their pieces to be photographed.

Special thanks to Michael, William and Ralph Harris-Brown; Julie Hill; Clive Parks, Kathrin Van-Spyk, and Shuna Harwood (www.casarotto.co.uk); Philip Parfitt of Wardrobe (01273 202201); Thomas von Nordheim (www.vonnordheim.com); Simon Phillips and Ewa J. Lind (www.mckinneymacartney.com); Lorna Green (020 7635 5157); Rokit; Radio Days: Cenci; Pop Boutique; Sandy Stagg of The Antique Clothing Company; and Lionel Segal of the Gallery of Antique Costume and Textiles.

Key

b bottom; *t* top; *l* left; *r* right; *c* centre
(ACC) Antique Clothing Company
(BA) Bridgeman Art Library
(Ce) Cenci
(CH) Carol Harris
(CHU) Church Street Antiques
(GACT) Gallery of Antique Costume & Textiles
(FC) First Call
(HD) Hulton-Deutsh Collection
(JM) Judith More
(JP) Joanna Proops
(LB) Linda Bee
(Lo) The Loft
(ML) Museum of London
(Ob) Observatory
(OPG) Octopus Publishing Group Ltd
(PB) Pop Boutique
(QB) Quite Bizarre
(RD) Radio Days
(S) Sotheby's, London
(SM) Sparkle Moore
(SPEL) Simon Phillips & Ewa J. Lind
(ST) Steve Tanner
(STo) Steinberg & Tolkien
(TR) Tim Ridley
(V&A) Victoria & Albert Museum
(Wa) Wardrobe

Front cover *c* OPG/TR/MM; Front cover *tl* OPG/TR/Nikki Lynes; Front cover, *tr* OPG/ST/CH; Front cover, *br* OPG/Ian Booth/Private Collection; Front cover, *br* OPG/ST/CH; Back cover, *tl* OPG/TR/SM; Back cover, *tr* OPG/ST/Ob; Back cover, *br* OPG/ST/CH; Front flap OPG/ST/Lorna Green; Back flap, *t* OPG/ST/CH; Back flap, *b* OPG/TR/Alfie's; 1 OPG/ST/CH; 3 OPG/ST/Thomas von Nordheim 4 *t* OPG/ST/CH; 4 *b* OPG/ST/CH; 5 *t* OPG/ST/QB; 5 *bl* OPG/TR/STo; 5 *br* OPG/ST/Lucy Parissi; 8 Corbis UK Ltd/HD; 9 Rex Features/Massey; 10 Millers/Echoes; 11 *l* ML; 11 *r* OPG/ST/CH; 11 *c* OPG/TR/Sotheby's,London; 12 OPG/ST/Wa; 13 *l* OPG/ST/FC; 13 *r* OPG/ST/FC; 14 *l* OPG/ST/FC; 14 *r* OPG/ST/FC; 15 *l* OPG/ST/FC; 15 *r* OPG/ST/Buffalo Shoes; 15 *c* OPG/ST/FC; 16 Corbis UK Ltd/HD; 18 *t* OPG/ST/ACC; 18 *b* OPG/ST/GACT; 19 *l* OPG/ST/ACC; 19 *tr* OPG/ST/ACC; 19 *br* OPG/ST/GACT; 20 *l* V&A; 20 *tr* OPG/ST/ACC; 20 *br* Millers/Echoes; 21 *l* OPG/ST/ACC; 21 *r* V&A; 22 *t* OPG/ST/GACT; 22 *b* BA; 23 *r* BA; 23 *t l* OPG/ST/Wa; 23 *c* Millers/LB; 23 *bl* OPG/ST/GACT; 24 *t* Millers/Echoes; 24 *b* Millers/CHU; 25 *r* ML; 25 *t l* ML; 25 *tr* ML; 25 *bl* Millers/Echoes; 26 *t* OPG/ST/JM; 26 *b* Millers/Echoes; 27 *tl* Millers/Echoes; 27 *tr* Millers/Echoes; 27 *cl* OPG/ST/JM; 27 *cr* Millers/CHU; 27 *bl* OPG/ST/Wa; 27 *br* OPG/ST/Wa; 28 *t* V&A; 28 *b* Millers/JP/Echoes; 29 *l* OPG/TR/S; 29 *r* V&A; 30 Corbis UK Ltd/HD; 32 *t* OPG/ST/CH; 32 *b* OPG/ST/CH; 33 *t* OPG/ST/CH; 33 *c* OPG/ST/CH; 33 *b* OPG/ST/CH; 34 *l* OPG/ST/CH; 34 *tr* OPG/ST/CH; 34 *br* OPG/ST/CH; 35 *tl* OPG/ST/CH; 35 *tr* OPG/ST/CH; 35 *b* OPG/ST/CH; 36 *t* Millers/JP/Echoes; 36 *bl* OPG/STCH; 36 *br* OPG/STCH; 37 *t* OPG/ST/CH; 37 *bl* OPG/ST/CH; 37 *br* OPG/ST/CH; 38 *t* OPG/ST/CH; 38 *b* OPG/ST/CH; 39 *t* OPG/ST/CH; 39 *c* OPG/ST/CH; 39 *b* OPG/ST/CH; 40 *t* OPG/ST/CH; 40 *b* OPG/ST/CH; 41 *t* OPG/ST/CH; 41 *c* OPG/ST/CH; 41 *bl* OPG/ST/CH; 41 *br* OPG/ST/CH; 42 *t* OPG/ST/FC; 42 *b* OPG/ST/FC; 43 *l* OPG/ST/FC; 43 *tr* OPG/ST/FC; 43 *br* OPG/ST/FC; 44 Conde Nast Publications Ltd/Hoyningen-Huene; 46 *t* OPG/ST/CH; 46 *b* OPG/ST/CH; 47 *tl* OPG/ST/CH; 47 *tr* OPG/ST/CH; 47 *cl* OPG/ST/CH; 47 *cr* OPG/ST/CH; 47 *b* OPG/ST/CH; 48 *t* OPG/ST/CH; ;48 *bl* OPG/ST/CH; 48 *br* OPG/ST/CH; 49 *t* OPG/ST/CH; 49 *c* OPG/ST/CH; 49 *b* OPG/ST/CH; 50 *tl* OPG/ST/CH; 50 *tr* OPG/ST/CH; 50 *b* OPG/ST/CH; 51 *tl* OPG/ST/CH; 51 *tr* OPG/ST/CH; 51 *c* OPG/ST/CH; 51 *b* OPG/ST/CH; 52 *t* OPG/ST/CH; 52 *c* OPG/ST/CH; 52 *b* OPG/ST/CH; 53 *tl* OPG/ST/CH; 53 *tr* OPG/ST/CH; 53 *c* OPG/ST/CH; 53 *b* OPG/ST/CH; 53 *br* OPG/ST/CH; 54 *t* OPG/ST/CH; 54 *bl* OPG/ST/CH; 54 *br* OPG/ST/CH; 55 *t* OPG/ST/CH; 55 *cl* OPG/ST/CH; 55 *cr* OPG/ST/CH; 55 *b* OPG/ST/CH; 56 *t* OPG/ST/FC; 56 *b* OPG/ST/FC; 57 *l* OPG/ST/FC; 57 *tr* OPG/TR/S; 57 *br* OPG/ST/FC; 58 Corbis UK Ltd/Bettman; 60 *t* OPG/ST/CH; 60 *b* OPG/ST/CH; 61 *t*, 61 *c* and 61 *b* all OPG/ST/SPEL; 62 *t* OPG/ST/SPEL; 62 *c* OPG/ST/SPEL; 62 *b* OPG/ST/CH; 63 *t* OPG/ST/SPEL; 63 *c* OPG/ST/SPEL; 63 *b* OPG/ST/FC; 64 *t* OPG/ST/FC; 64 *b* OPG/ST/CH; 65 *tl* OPG/ST/FC; 65 *tr* OPG/ST/Wa; 65 *bl* OPG/ST/FC; 65 *br* OPG/ST/FC; 66 *t* OPG/ST/CH; 66 *b* Millers/CH; 67 *t* OPG/ST/CH; 67 *c* Millers/CH; 67 *b* OPG/ST/Wa; 68 *t* OPG/ST/CH; 68 *b* OPG/ST/SPEL; 69 *tl* OPG/ST/SPEL; 69 *tr* OPG/ST/SPEL; 69 *tl* OPG/ST/SPEL; 69 *c* OPG/ST/SPEL; 69 *bl* OPG/ST/CH; 69 *br* OPG/ST/CH; 70 *tl* OPG/ST/SPEL; 70 *tr* OPG/ST/SPEL; 70 *b* OPG/ST/SPEL; 71 *t* OPG/ST/SPEL; 71 *c* OPG/ST/SPEL; 71 *b* OPG/ST/CH; 72 Corbis UK Ltd/HD; 74 *t* OPG/TR/SM; 74 *b* OPG/TR/MM; 75 *t* OPG/ST/FC; 75 *c* OPG/TR/MM; 75 *b* OPG/ST/FC; 76 *t* OPG/TR/SM; 76 *c* OPG/ST/FC; 76 *b* OPG/ST/FC; 77 *t* OPG/ST/FC; 77 *c* OPG/TR/SM; 77 *b* OPG/ST/FC; 78 *t* OPG/TR/SM; 78 *b* OPG/ST/FC; 79 *t* OPG/ST/FC; 79 *c* OPG/ST/FC; 79 *b* OPG/ST/FC; 80 *t* OPG/ST/FC; 80 *b* OPG/ST/CH; 81 *tl* OPG/ST/FC; 81 *tr* OPG/TR/SM; 81 *b* OPG/TR/MM; 82 *t* OPG/ST/FC; 82 *b* OPG/TR/STo; 83 *t* OPG/TR/STo; 83 *c* OPG/TR/LB; 83 *b* OPG/Ian Booth/Alfie's; 84 *t* OPG/TR/SM; 84 *b* OPG/ST/FC; 85 *tl* OPG/TR/SM; 85 *tr* OPG/TR/SM; 85 *cl* OPG/ST/FC; 85 *cr* OPG/ST/FC; 85 *b* OPG/ST/FC; 86 Advertising Archives; 88 *t* OPG/ST/FC; 88 *b* OPG/ST/FC; 89 *t* OPG/ST/FC; 89 *cl* OPG/TR/Nikki Lynes; 89 *cr* OPG/ST/FC; 89 *b* OPG/ST/FC; 90 *t* OPG/ST/FC; 90 *c* OPG/ST/FC; 90 *b* OPG/ST/FC; 91 *tl* OPG/ST/Ob; 91 *tr* OPG/ST/FC; 91 *b* OPG/ST/FC; 92 *t* OPG/ST/FC; 92 *b* OPG/TR/Alfie's; 93 *tl* OPG/TR/STo; 93 *tr* OPG/ST/CH; 93 *b* OPG/ST/FC; 94 *t* OPG/ST/Ce; 94 *b* OPG/ST/FC; 95 *tl* OPG/TR/RD; 95 *tr* OPG/ST/Ce; 95 *bl* OPG/ST/Ce; 95 *br* OPG/TR/RD; 96 *t* OPG/ST/FC; 96 *b* OPG/TR/STo; 97 *tl* OPG/TR/Alfie's; 97 *tr* OPG/TR/Nikki Lynes; 97 *c* OPG/TR/RD; 97 *b* OPG/Target Gallery; 98 *t* OPG/TR/Nikki Lynes; 98 *b* OPG/TR/RD; 99 *t* OPG/ST/FC; 99 *b* OPG/Ob; 100 Corbis UK Ltd/HD; 102 *t* OPG/ST/FC; 102 *b* OPG/ST/FC; 103 *t* OPG/ST/FC; 103 *c* OPG/ST/FC; 103 *b* OPG/ST/FC; 104 *l* OPG/ST/FC; 104 *t* OPG/ST/FC; 104 *b* OPG/ST/FC; 105 *l* OPG/ST/FC; 105 *tr* OPG/ST/FC; 105 *br* OPG/ST/FC; 106 *t* OPG/ST/Ob; 106 *c* OPG/ST/Lorna Green; 106 *b* OPG/ST/Lorna Green; 107 *r* OPG/ST/Ob; 107 *tl* OPG/ST/Ob; 107 *t c* OPG/ST/Ob; 107 *bl* OPG/ST/RD; 108 *t* OPG/ST/FC; 108 *b* OPG/ST/Ce; 109 *tl* OPG/ST/Ce; 109 *tr* OPG/ST/Ce; 109 *b* OPG/ST/FC; 110 *t* OPG/ST/FC; 110 *b* OPG/ST/FC; 111 *t* OPG/ST/FC; 111 *c* OPG/ST/FC; 111 *b* OPG/ST/FC; 112 *t* OPG/ST/FC; 112 *b* OPG/ST/FC; 113 *r* OPG/ST/FC; 113 *tl* OPG/ST/FC; 113 *b* OPG/ST/FC; 114 *t* OPG/ST/Rokit; 115 *t* OPG/ST/FC; 115 *c* OPG/ST/FC; 115 *b* OPG/ST/FC; 116 Advertising Archives/Escada; 118 *t* OPG/ST/Ob; 118 *b* OPG/ST/FC; 119 *t* OPG/ST/FC; 119 *b* OPG/ST/Ob; 120 *t* OPG/ST; 120 *c* OPG/ST/FC; 120 *b* OPG/ST/FC; 121 *tl* OPG/ST/Ob; 121 *tr* OPG/ST/FC; 121 *b* OPG/ST/FC; 122 *t* OPG/ST/FC; 122 *b* OPG/ST/FC; 123 *t* OPG/ST/Ob; 123 *bl* OPG/ST/Ob; 123 *br* OPG/ST/FC; 124 *tl* OPG/ST/CH; 124 *tr* OPG/ST/CH; 124 *bl* OPG/ST/CH; 124 *br* OPG/ST/CH; 125 *tl* OPG/ST/CH; 125 *tr* OPG/ST/CH; 125 *cr* OPG/ST/FC; 125 *bl* OPG/ST/CH; 125 *br* OPG/ST/CH; 126 *tl* OPG/ST/JM; 126 *tr* OPG/ST/FC; 126 *bl* OPG/ST/FC; 126 *br* OPG/ST/FC; 127 *t* Millers/Identity; 127 *c* OPG/ST/PB; 127 *b* OPG/ST/PB; 128 *t* OPG/ST/FC; 128 *b* OPG/ST/QB; 129 *tl* OPG/ST/FC; 129 *tr* OPG/ST/Ob; 129 *br* OPG/ST/PB; 130 *t* OPG/ST/Ob; 130 *b* OPG/ST/PB; 131 *tl* OPG/ST/PB; 131 *tr* OPG/ST/QB; 131 *bl* OPG/ST/PB; 131 *br* OPG/ST/Gaelle Lochner; 132 Chris Moore Ltd; 134 *t* OPG/ST/JM; 134 *b* OPG/ST/JM; 135 *tl* OPG/ST/Lo; 135 *tr* OPG/ST/Thomas von Nordheim; 135 *b* OPG/ST/Lo; 136 *tl* OPG/ST/Ob; 136 *bl* OPG/ST/Lo; 137 *t* OPG/ST/Lo; 137 *c* OPG/ST/Lo; 137 *b* OPG/ST/Lo; 138 *b* OPG/ST/Lo; 139 *r* OPG/ST/Lo; 139 *tl* OPG/ST/Lucy Parissi; 139 *bl* OPG/ST/Lo; 140 *t* OPG/ST; 140 *b* OPG/ST; 141 *t* OPG/ST/Vicky Short; 141 *c* OPG/ST; 141 *b* OPG/ST/Lucy Parissi; 142 *t* OPG/ST/Lorna Green; 142 *b* OPG/ST/Lucy Parissi; 143 *tl* OPG/ST/JM; 143 *tr* OPG/ST; 143 *c* OPG/ST/Buffalo Shoes; 143 *br* OPG/Ian Booth/Private Collection; 144 *t* OPG/ST; 144 *b* OPG/ST; 145 *tr* OPG/Wa; 145 *c* OPG/ST; 145 *b* OPG/ST/CH; 146 *t* OPG/ST/Ob; 146 *b* OPG/ST; 147 *t* OPG/ST/William Brown; 147 *bl* OPG/ST; 147 *b c* OPG/ST; 147 *br* OPG/ST/Dan Newman